DESERVING MERCY

Careless decisions.
Harsh consequences.

Ludrick "Rell C" Cooper

Deserving Mercy
Copyright © 2019 by Ludrick "Rell C" Cooper

All rights reserved. No part of this publication may be reproduced, distributed, or transmitted in any form or by any means, including photocopying, recording, or other electronic or mechanical methods, without the prior written permission of the author, except in the case of brief quotations embodied in critical reviews and certain other non-commercial uses permitted by copyright law.

Disclaimer: This story is inspired by a true story. Therefore, the characters, places, and certain things have been changed and/or altered to protect those individuals portrayed in this novel. No intentions are to defame anyone or thing.

Tellwell Talent
www.tellwell.ca

ISBN
978-0-2288-1475-7 (Hardcover)
978-0-2288-1474-0 (Paperback)
978-0-2288-1476-4 (eBook)

Table of Contents

Acknowledgements v
Introduction vii
The History of Bazemore College ix
Definitions xi

Chapter 1	How it All Started	1
Chapter 2	Falsely Accused	5
Chapter 3	Breaking the Bad News	9
Chapter 4	Out on Bail	13
Chapter 5	The Truth Hurts	17
Chapter 6	The Hearing	22
Chapter 7	To Appeal	26
Chapter 8	Suspended from College	29
Chapter 9	A Free Vacation at Donovan's Place	32
Chapter 10	The Second Court Visit	36
Chapter 11	The Next Semester	40
Chapter 12	Probation: The First Half	43
Chapter 13	Probation: The Final Half	49
Chapter 14	Closer to Graduation	54
Chapter 15	Jamal and Terri	58
Chapter 16	Gearing Up for Graduation	61
Chapter 17	The County Jail Visit	65
Chapter 18	Life After Bazemore College	68
Chapter 19	Film School, Unemployment Benefits, and a Pardon	70

Chapter 20 The Pardon Hearing 73
Chapter 21 Deserving Mercy 77

Deserving Mercy's Short Book of Poetry:
Poetry inspired by this story 79
About the Book 83

Acknowledgements

First and foremost, I'd like to thank God who is the head of my life and the Creator of the Heavens and Earth. Without you, nothing is possible.

Next, I'd like to thank my beautiful wife Kimberly. Thank you for your motivation. This book would not be possible without you either.

Lastly, I'd like to thank my immediate family. My parents for bringing me into this world, teaching me morals, and for the financial assistance. To my big sis, Aisha, thanks for all of your support and making me a great uncle for my nephew (Armon) and niece (Amber). I love you all.

Introduction

This story is based on a short film I created in 2016 while residing in Orlando, Florida. The short film, which is also entitled *Deserving Mercy*, is loosely based on a true story that took place on the campus of a Historically Black College and/or University (HBCU). This short film can be found on YouTube. This story is something many young adults can learn from. It is especially relevant to high school students and those thinking about attending college.

  I received a lot of inspiration to write this novel while enrolled at Webster University as a Master of Arts in English Education grad student. While taking the course Teaching Writing, my desire and drive to write awakened. Also, while taking Young Adult Literature, I was inspired by several of the books we were instructed to read. I knew that *Deserving Mercy* the film was a lesson that many young adults would learn from so I decided to put it into writing as well.

The History of Bazemore College

Bazemore College is an HBCU in the South. It was founded by the late Colonel Samuel Bazemore in 1866. Bazemore, who was a surviving soldier that fought in the Civil War for the North. After the war, he and his family purchased 250 acres of land to build his home and a new school for the freed slaves in the area. Before being named Bazemore College, it was called Bazemore Institute For the New Freed Slaves. He served as the first president for 20 years until his death.

His younger brother, Daniel Bazemore was appointed the next president. That same year, the name was changed to Bazemore College. The college began to focus more on teaching students how to become educators to teach more black youth.

Today, Bazemore College has 70 different majors with over 3,000 students. It is ranked #2 as the best private HBCU in the U.S. according to the National Black School Magazine. However, since the college has enforced an "Open Enrollment," it has attracted many students from different backgrounds. Although, the college is located in one of the most crime infested areas of the country, it still manages to sustain their accreditation and maintain a successful graduation rate. Many have argue that the college needs to do something to decrease crime and get rid of all the negative stereotypes. Despite all of the negative publicity, the school still manages to produce successful graduates making Bazemore College one of the most well rounded colleges in the country.

Definitions

Mercy| a blessing that is an act of divine favor or compassion.
Pardon| a release from the legal penalties of an offense.
Expunge| to cancel out or destroy completely.

Chapter One

HOW IT ALL STARTED

It was a very dull cloudy day on the campus of Bazemore College, the fall semester of 2002 to be exact. Jamal was bored. All of his friends on campus were either working or as bored as he was. His roommate, Craig, had gotten lucky and landed a paid internship with an insurance company, so Jamal had the room to himself most evenings. So after class, it's usually to the caf, to the computer lab, then to the dorm room. Well, this particular evening, he ran into Kris.

"Yo what's up, Jamal?"

"Nothing much," Jamal said. "Just about to watch TV all night. What What you got going on?"

"It's Ty's birthday," he said.

"Oh word?" said Jamal.

"Yeah, I'm headed to the liquor store now. You know anyone 21 or older?" Kris asked.

"Nah," Jamal replied.

"Well, hopefully I can find someone at the store old enough, but we should have some liquor and weed later tonight. Come through."

"That's a bet," Jamal said as he continued walking to the Hazelwood Street Dormitory.

Jamal got on his laptop inside his dorm room and did some reading till that got old. He watched tv, but nothing good was on except music videos. He'd seen all the latest movie re-runs.

"I really don't feel like going, but I'll at least show my face," he said to himself. Jamal was the kind of person who got along with everyone. His well-rounded and non judgement behavior allowed him to be respected from many peers. However, this type of personality sometimes attracted the wrong crowd. Many people felt comfortable being around him. Therefore, sometimes they felt like they could casually manipulate him while still being a friend if that makes sense. But Jamal didn't mind being by himself sometimes. In fact, he enjoyed his space.

Jamal went down to the second floor to Kris and Ty's room. When he got there he was greeted by other classmates.

"What's up Ty? Happy birthday!"

"Man I appreciate that bro," Ty replied.

Someone passed Jamal a cup with straight vodka, no chaser. All the guys in the room were high from marijuana and buzzed from sipping vodka. One of the guys, Bilal who spoke with a thick *geechee*[1] accent, suggested that since Jamal had arrived, they should all put their weed together to roll a bigger blunt so they can really get high.

"We can't smoke in here anymore. I don't want to make the weed smoke obvious," said Ty.

Bilal replied, "We can't smoke up in my room! My room too hot! Aye Jamal, way yo roommate at? Let us smoke in yo room".

"My roommate gone, but okay," Jamal said.

"Yeah let's smoke in your room," said Kris.

Minutes later, the guys were all in Jamal's room having a good time. Music was playing and the guys began freestyling to some rap music beats. They argued about who was the best hip hop lyricist of all time. Jamal said his favorite lyricist of all time was, Nas. Kris favorite was Jay-Z. Bilal said his favorite was Lil Wayne. Another guy in the room from Brooklyn, which is what everyone on campus calls him, said his favorites were Biggie, Hov, Jadakiss, and Fabolous. They all laughed at him since every artist he mentioned was from New York.

"Yall must forgot where hip-hop started", said Brooklyn. I bet New York rappers can't rap like this tho," said Bilal as he played a classic hip hop song, *Still Smoking* by Mystikal. Coincidentally, this song was about smoking marijuana and the artist talked about how he was smoking weed

---

[1] term used of the Gullah dialect, or a speaker of this dialect which is mainly spoken by descendants of African slaves in the Low Country region of South Carolina.

in a hotel room and someone (who he thought was security) knocked on the door. But while in Jamal's room, luckily they were no longer smoking anymore.

JB came knocking on the door like a cop and startled the guys. As they opened the door for him, he mentioned that he could smell smoke heavily from his room, but the guys were so high they ignored him. "Yall got this whole hallway smelling like weed", said JB. All Jamal did was spray a little air freshener.

One of the RAs smelled marijuana smoke coming from the room also. He reported this to the dorm director, Mr Phillps. Mr Phillips went up to the third floor. As soon as he got to the third floor, he could tell where the scent of marijuana smoke was coming from. He knocked on Jamal's door. At first, they didn't pay any attention to it, but then the second time he knocked, all their eyes shifted to the door. They hoped it was another friend and no one else. Kris looked through the peephole and saw who it was.

"Oh snap, it's Mr Phillips!" he exclaimed in a hushed voice. Jamal panicked and desperately lit up a cigarette to get rid of the weed smell. It was best to have the room smell like cigarettes than instead of marijuana. He took a quick puff and then threw it out of the window. Assuming that all the evidence was gone, Jamal remained calm.

Since no one opened the door, Mr Phillips forcefully opened it himself with his own set of dorm director master keys. He then walks in.

"No one heard me knocking?" he said. "Then he asks, "Who's room is this"?

"Mines", Jamal replied.

"Let me see your ID. As a matter of fact, let me see everyone's ID", said Mr. Phillips.

"Alright guys, I know the smell of marijuana smoke. Campus public safety are on their way here. So if you guys have anything on you, you're going to be in big trouble," Mr Phillips said.

Because it was normal at Bazemore College, Jamal didn't think he'd be in any serious trouble. Just last semester, there was a huge drug bust in the football team's dormitory. Twelve players were caught drug trafficking, but they avoided arrest charges, stayed in school and continued being a part of the football program. The entire incident was swept under the rug obviously because they were athletes and brought in a lot of money for the school. Just a week before, one of his classmates was caught in another dorm with some other friends smoking marijuana, and a particular dorm director let them go as well. Jamal felt this would be no different.

The public safety officers finally arrived along with several other security guards.

"Sorry, we're a little late. There was an incident where a student poured urine out the window on another student," said Officer Emerson. The officers and guards began their search. Brooklyn was caught with a substantial amount of weed on him. He had nowhere to hide it since he was dressed in basketball gear. Jamal could see from the corner of his eyes and was in shock. One of the officers escorted Jamal outside onto the hallway. He was last to be searched.

He was still nervous, but confident that he did nothing wrong except for allowing the guys into his room. After the officers were done searching him, he was cleared. They found no drugs on Jamal and none on the guys other than Brooklyn. The officers further searched the room. Later, one of the officers, Officer Brooks, walked up to Jamal.

"Does this belong to you?" asked Officer Brooks, with a big bag of weed and three small individual bags inside.

"No sir, that's not mine," Jamal answered.

"Well, whose is it?" Officer Brooks asked.

"I don't know sir, but it's not mine," Jamal replied.

"Understand this, if no one claims this, you're coming with us", said Officer Brooks.

He turns to the rest of the guys and asks them. Each one denies it.

"Alright, put your hands behind your back", said Officer Brooks.

He handcuffs Jamal and escorts him as well as Brooklyn outside behind the dormitory so no one can see them.

Chapter Two

FALSELY ACCUSED

The officers escorted the two gentlemen behind the dormitory so no one would see them. They were placed inside the public safety vehicle.

"Wow, an arrest on my first day on the job," said Officer Wright.

"Welcome to the force," Officer Brooks replied. Jamal and Brooklyn have a whispered discussion.

"You didn't have anything to do with this," Brooklyn said to Jamal.

"I know right. This feels like a bad dream". The officers heard their conversation but ignored it. They got to the campus public safety headquarters building for more questioning and paperwork.

"They're probably going to let us go," Jamal told Brooklyn.

"What makes you think that?" he asked Jamal.

"You know how many I seen this happen before"?

More officers were inside headquarters as they entered the building. The officers who made the arrest lets the head chief know what happened.

"Good job Officer Emerson", said the head chief. Jamal and Brooklyn both looked at each other. Officer Emerson was the only white officer employed by the HBCU who initiated the order for the two to be arrested in the first place. The officers explained to the guys that they have to take them to the county jail due to the amount of drugs that were found in their possession. They were both escorted to the county jail.

Jamal wished this was a dream. Was this really is happening?

"The only person who can get us out of this is God," Jamal said.

"I still can't believe one of those dudes hid that weed in your pillow and didn't claim it", said Brooklyn.

"I can't believe it either. Let's pray", Jamal responded. Both Jamal and Brooklyn bowed their heads while Jamal led in prayer:

> *Dear Heavenly Father, forgive us for we know not what we did. Lord forgive the gentleman who left the weed in my pillow. Whomever he may be. Lord help us forgive. Even the RA and dorm director who were only doing their job. Lord allow us to forgive the officers who believes that I'm innocent or guilty. Humble me as I take this sacrifice and let your will be done. Not mines. Let the conviction have its way through the men who could've helped me. Last but not least, Lord only allow me to bear whatever I can. Thank you Father for it is already being done. Amen.*

"This is yall's first charge right", asked Officer Brooks.
"Yeah", said Jamal Brooklyn.
"Okay, once you guys get bailed out and whenever your court date is, remember to apply for PTI. That stands for Pre-Trial Intervention. It's a program where you do community service and have some counseling. Once you're finish, the charge won't show up on your record. I'm going to recommend you two for it", said Officer Brooks.

When they finally got to booking, they saw a patty wagon filled with young black men in handcuffs. This reminded them of slavery. They were so nervous. They couldn't wait to be uncuffed and booked so they could use the restroom. Luckily, both of the guys were in the same holding cell room together at the officer's request.

"This is so crazy," Jamal said.
"This is beyond crazy", Brooklyn stated.
"All I wanted to do was show Ty some love on his birthday and this is what happens. Who you think hid that weed in my pillow," said Jamal.
"Honestly speaking, I don't really know. But if I had to guess, I would say Ty," said Brooklyn.

Jamal thought about it. Ty was sitting close by his pillow on his bed. It all made sense, but at the moment Jamal had to figure his way out of this situation first. Andre got escorted into the room by officers. As soon as he stepped foot inside the cell and began talking, Brooklyn recognized his accent and presumed he was from up north, like him.

"Where you from?" he asked. "Jersey."

"You from up top too?"

"Yeah, Brooklyn", said Brooklyn.

"What you doing in here?" he asked Brooklyn.

"Possession with the intent to distribute".

"What about you?" Brooklyn asked.

"I was hanging outside with my cousins in the parking lot drinking and neighbors decided to call the cops on us. Only thing they could get me for was underage drinking.

"Hopefully, I'll be out on a PR bond," he said.

"What's a PR bond?" Jamal asked.

"It's a bond where I won't have to pay 10% of my bail. I'll be out without having to pay anything at all," he said.

"Well, I hope we get one," said Jamal.

"It depends on how serious the crime is and based on what everyone else charges are during bond court", he explained.

The guys finally got the chance to make their phone calls inside the commons area of the detention center. There were plenty of enough phones for inmates to use and not have to do any long waiting. Jamal decided to wait until he knows the outcome of his bond before he notified his parents. He called Kris and Ty's dorm room. Kris answered. Without any greeting, Jamal asked,

"Be honest with me. Who put that weed in my pillow"?

"I'm trying to figure that out myself. You alright up in there though", replied Kris, trying to deflect Jamal's question.

"I have a lot on my mind right now and I don't belong in here", said Jamal.

"Well, I'll find out for you who did it", be safe, said Kris.

Aight, talk to you later", said Jamal. Jamal hung up the phone, walked over to an available seat and sat down as he waited to be called back into their holding cells.

During the phone call time, Jamal got the chance to speak with someone else who was also held in custody.

"Hey this your first time in here?" Steve asked Jamal. Steve was some random inmate who stays in and out of county jail and prison.

"Yeah, what about you?" Jamal replied.

"Nah, but you should be good if this your first time though. They'll give you a PR bond", he said.

"Really?" said Jamal.

"Trust me, I know. I've been locked up so many times. I wish this was my first time," he said.

This calmed Jamal and made him feel a little better. If he could get a PR bond, he would not have to let his parents know what happened. At least that's what he was thinking.

Phone call and recess time was over. The guys were ordered back to their assigned holding cell rooms. Walks in, Jonathan who had on no shoes, just socks on his feet. They all stared at his feet whispering about why he doesn't have any shoes on.

He goes, "I was running from the police".

Brooklyn asks, "Why were you running?"

Jonathan answered, "I stole a car."

An officer came inside the cell to give him a pair of sandals. The cell room is about 12 feet in length, with a toilet, and a cement bench that can barely fit all four of the inmates. The guys talked for hours and hours till they fell asleep, uncomfortably. They literally had to sleep while sitting on the cement bench with their arms folded on their legs and their heads resting on their arms.

Bond court was held at 8:00 a.m. By six o'clock, another inmate was lead in, but there was no room for him on the cement bench. You could smell the alcohol on him as he stepped in the cell. He looked at the guys and sat on the floor.

Breakfast was served, but Jamal, Brooklyn, and Andre had no appetite to eat. The other two inmates took theirs instead. The guys were anxious to get out of jail. The bond court judge had little to no patience whatsoever. All he wanted to hear in response to his questions were "yes sir" or "no sir."

"I don't understand 'uh huh.' I don't know what that means...and take your hands out of your pockets" he told one man who was charged for selling crack-cocaine while violating his parole.

Andre was able to get a PR bond with his charge.

Jamal was nervous.

Chapter Three

BREAKING THE BAD NEWS

Jamal was silently and nervously praying again as the judge called him to the stand.

"Keep your hands out of your pockets," said the bailiff/officer.

Jamal was thinking how difficult that was going to be since his pants were a little baggy and his belt was taken away from him during booking.

His charge was read out loud like everyone else's.

"Jamal Williams. Charged with possession of marijuana with the intent to distribute and within a school. Oh, so you're a drug dealer", the judge asked.

Jamal answered back, "No sir, I am not."

"What kind of work you do", asked the judge.

"I'm a college student", answered Jamal.

"What school do you attend", the judge asked.

"Bazemore College", said Jamal

"Why I'm not surprised", the judge mumbled.

Next, he tells Jamal, "You get a surety bond of $2000. Be sure to call your parents so they can bail you out. Your official court date is one month from today. Next!", said the judge.

Filled with disappointment, this meant Jamal had to call his parents to notify them of his bond, which was $2000, but he can pay just 10% with a bond bailsman. The same went for Brooklyn, except his bond was $3000 because of his out of state ID that was discovered during booking. Andre was released moments later. You could tell he was happy to get a PR bond.

All of the other inmates had time again to make their phone calls and recess from their assigned cells. Jamal was patiently and nervously waiting and praying. It was finally time for him to make his phone calls. First, he called his dorm room and Craig picked up. Jamal was thankful that he answered.

"Hello", answered Craig.

"Hey this Jamal, can you do me a favor?" Jamal asked.

"Sure, anything. I heard what happened," Craig replied.

"There's a yellow manilla folder on my desk. On the folder is a toll free number written, which is the number to my dad's office. Let me know what that number is so I can call and let him know," Jamal explained.

"Sure thing", Craig replied. Craig gave him the number and they both hung up.

Repeating the number to himself while dialing the number to his dad's office, Jamal took one deep breath. The receptionist answered and forwarded Jamal to his dad's office phone. His voicemail message came on instead.

As soon as Jamal began talking, he couldn't help but to cry out to his father.

"Dad this is Jamal! Something horrible happened to me last night. I allowed some friends in my dorm room. Long story short, we had weed, but one of them left some in my pillow and I got charged for it! I'm in jail and I need you to come get me out. I don't belong here", cried out Jamal.

Lunch was served, but again, Jamal and Brooklyn had no appetite. They gave their lunches away to the other inmates, but ate the fruit instead.

Jamal's father, who's a social worker for Brownman county, got back to his office at work and played his voicemail messages. He listened to Jamal's message, replayed it again, closed the door and then stormed out of his office.

"I have a family emergency. It's my son", said Mr Williams to one of the secretaries.

Jamal's dad traveled an hour and half to get to the detention center. He had to locate a bail bondsman first as he was so much in a rush that he didn't remember what Jamal said in the voicemail message.

Brooklyn was unable to get in touch with his parents. The detention center inmates could only make local phone calls. He let his roommate know what was going on. He tried calling his parents collect, but couldn't get anyone just yet.

Jamal's dad finally located a bondsman. It wasn't hard at all to find a bondsman. There were plenty of businesses like these the closer you got to the Detention Center. Mr Williams quickly walked inside of the bondsman building.

"How can I help you sir", asked the bondsman clerk.

"Yes, I need to get my son out of jail as soon as possible", said Mr Williams.

He gave them all of the necessary information to process Jamal's paperwork for bail. Next, a bondsman agent came and visited Jamal to get his signature and this cheered him up a little bit. In fact, this was the best news he gotten in the past twelve hours. Not wanting to gloat in front of Brooklyn, Jamal remained humbled and just encouraged him.

"I'll be spending the night, I guess, until my mom wires the money to a bondsman here", he said to Jamal.

"You need any favors once I get back on campus?" asked Jamal.

"Just let everyone know I'll be out by tomorrow," Brooklyn said.

The two gives each other dap as a correctional officer escorted Brooklyn to be dressed in an inmate uniform.

It appeared that God answered Jamal's prayers.

"Any update on my release sir", asked Jamal to one of officers working inside the jail.

"What's your name", asked the officer.

"Jamal Williams", replied Jamal.

"Should be real soon son. Good thing is just know you're getting out", said the officer. Jamal says to the officer,

"I don't belong here".

"You're not the only one my friend", the officer said.

Seem like time is moving slow. Being in jail gives him all the time in world to think about his consequences.

"Williams", called out by one of the officers.

"Yes", asked Jamal.

"You're good to go. Come step inside this room here", said the officer.

There, he still ends up waiting for about another 45 minutes or so. It seems like the officers were just taking their time on purpose to release him. Another officer ordered him to finalize his paperwork at the releasing station. His belongings were returned. When Jamal got booked, he had about $7 on him. While he got released, his money was returned to him, but in the form of all coins. Jamal couldn't believe it. He was finally free from county jail. Looking for his father, he sees him and gives him a big hug as tears automatically come down his face.

Chapter Four
OUT ON BAIL

"I didn't do this dad, this was a huge mistake," Jamal explained.

"I know, son. I know you didn't do anything. I believe you," said Mr Williams.

They hopped inside of his dad's truck to head over to the bail bondsman's office, which wasn't that far from the jail. They arrived and Jamal had more paperwork to fill out.

"You ought to be thankful for a good parent such as your dad to bail you out of jail," said the bail bondsman worker.

"I definitely am," said Jamal.

"Starting tomorrow morning, you will need to call our office every day to check in with us. If you miss three consecutive days without calling us before your court visit, your bond will be forfeited. They did explained to you about your court hearing right?" she asked.

"Yes mam", said Jamal.

Jamal and his father left the bail bondsman office. Trying to remember how to get back to campus as well as having a conversation about why Jamal was arrested.

"I cannot remember how to get back to Bazemore from here, do you", asked Mr Williams.

"The best way is to go towards SCU(South Carolina University) and the downtown area", said Jamal.

"So tell me the whole story son. What happened", asked Mr Williams.

"Well, I was invited to some friends room. It was Ty's birthday. We had a couple of drinks. Then, everyone suggested we go in my room to smoke.

After everything was said and done, the dorm director, Mr Phillips came and inspected the room. He called public safety. They searched me, found nothing. Evidently, one of the guys hid a substantial amount of weed in my pillow. No one claimed it. So they took me to jail for it", said Jamal.

"Wow, things sure have changed since I was in undergrad. I remember people would be smoking reefa all the time in their rooms, but no one would ever got in trouble for it. Sounds like to me they're trying to make an example out of you", said Mr Williams.

"I feel the same way", said Jamal.

"Just hope this small incident doesn't ruin the rest of your life", his father stated.

"Well, one of the officers at Bazemore said that I will need to apply for PTI", said Jamal.

"What's that", Mr Williams asked.

"It's supposed help remove the charge off my record", said Jamal.

"Okay, are you hungry", Mr Williams asked.

"Yes, I'm starving", said Jamal.

"Well, I'll take you to go get something to eat", said Mr Williams.

"Thanks, I didn't eat anything in there," Jamal said.

"What do you want to eat?" he asked.

"There's a chinese restaurant close by campus", said Jamal.

His dad took him to the chinese restaurant. Jamal came back with an order of shrimp fried rice and four whole chicken wings. Finally, they arrived on campus to Jamal's dormitory.

"You think your dorm director is there?" he asked Jamal.

He replied, "He should be".

They both get out of the vehicle and walked toward the entrance of the dorm. No one sees Jamal and his father. In fact, no one really knows what happened the night before. Headed towards Mr Phillips's office, but another student is speaking with him inside. The door was opened.

"I hate to interrupt, Mr Phillips, but this is my father, he'd like to speak with you" said Jamal.

"How you doing sir? If you could go upstairs to your room, I'll meet you up there in a few minutes", said Mr Phillips. Jamal and his dad go upstairs to Jamal's room.

While inside Jamal's room, Mr Williams asked Jamal, "So these guys are your friends?" "No they're not my friends. More like associates", replied Jamal.

"Do you know who hid the weed inside your pillow?" his dad asked.

"Not for sure, but I'm quite sure I will find out," said Jamal.

There was a knock on the door. It was Mr Phillips again. Mr Phillips explained his side of the story. He told Jamal's father that it came to his attention that the smell of marijuana smoke was coming from a room on Jamal's floor. During this inspection and observation, he came to Jamal's door and knocked. He said he heard talking, but no one never came to open the door. So he made it upon himself to eventually open the door and entered the room. He said there was no doubt that they had been smoking. The scent was very strong. He called campus safety. When they arrived, they searched all the guys, but only found drugs on one person, which was Brooklyn. They then searched Jamal's room and found a bag of marijuana hidden in his pillow.

"It didn't belong to me," Jamal stressed to Mr Phillips.

"I understand your frustration, but if these guys were your so called friends, they wouldn't have allowed you to go down for something you had nothing to do with", said Mr Phillips.

"He's right", said Mr Williams.

"In a few days, there will be a college hearing administered by the disciplinary board. It'll be somewhat like a court setting and would help Jamal's case if you could make it Mr Williams", said Mr Phillips.

"I will most definitely make it" said Mr Williams.

"It is also important that the person who left the drugs in his room to confess", said Mr Phillips.

As Mr Phillips turned to depart, Jamal's dad noticed the class ring he was wearing. "So you graduated from here, too," Mr Williams asked Mr Phillips.

"Why yes, class of 70. And you?" he asked.

"Class of 75", said Mr Williams.

"Well, it was nice meeting you, but unfortunately not on these terms", said Mr Phillips.

"Same here", said Mr Williams. Mr Phillips looked at Jamal and told him, "Watch who you hang around" as he exited Jamal's room.

"I'm sorry dad if I caused any trouble, but honestly I didn't know that any of these guys had that much amount of weed on them", said Jamal.

"Don't beat yourself up about it", said Mr Williams.

"You think mom is going to be okay when she finds out", asked Jamal.

"I don't know how I'm going to tell your mother when she wakes up in the morning", his dad said.

"Okay, I'll walk you outside", said Jamal.

As they walked to the outside, Jamal sees the same cops who were there when he was arrested. They spoke to his father to let him know that he would be eligible for PTI and that his record can be expunged. This was a relief for Jamal's dad.

Jamal went back up to his room. After being in Jail for close to 24 hours without a shower, he was ready for one. He went down the hallway to the restroom/shower. After he cleaned up, he went back to his dorm room to enjoy his chinese dinner. Craig comes in later.

"You're finally back, what's up Jamal?" said Craig.

"Man I'm so glad to be finally out. Nothing to do in jail but think about how to avoid it," said Jamal.

"That's so true, but let me tell you how messed up this room was", said Craig.

"Foreal?" Jamal asked.

"Everything was laid out on the floor. I had to make up both our beds, put everything back where they were", Craig explained.

"What I'm dying to know is who left weed in my pillow", he said.

"I have no idea bro", Craig replied.

"Well, the truth will come to light soon and I'm gonna find out", said Jamal. Jamal turned off the light and turned on his lamp as he finished his dinner and went to bed.

Chapter Five

THE TRUTH HURTS

After a good rest after being in jail, Jamal got up early to start his day. Craig was still asleep in his bed. As Jamal headed to the caf for breakfast, he ran into Bilal.

"Yo what happened the other night," asked Bilal.

"They took us to jail. What else?" Jamal replied.

"If I was you, I'd let Ty have it, that's word on my bubba. You feel me", said Bilal.

"Wait a minute, that's who left the weed in my pillow?" asked Jamal.

"Yeah, it was him. And the crazy thing is he was sitting right by your window. All had to do throw da bag out da window", Bilal stated.

"I tightened up my belt so fast when Mr Phillips opened your door… I had a whole ounce in my boxers! where Brooklyn at," asked Bilal.

"He should be out later. His bond was higher than mines since he from out of state", explained Jamal. "Wait, so you had weed on you and they didn't find it?", asked Jamal.

"A whole ounce", stated Bilal.

As the two go their separate ways, Jamal goes inside the caf. After getting his food and finding a seat to himself, Ty and Kris comes over to sit with him. Jamal gets up to sit somewhere else.

"Is everything good?", asked Kris as Jamal walks off. Kris follows behind Jamal.

"Why you acting like nothing happened the other night? They took us to county and I had to call my dad to bail me out. How do you think I'm supposed to feel?" asked Jamal.

"Look man, I know you upset, but he didn't mean to leave that weed in your pillow, seriously," Kris said in an attempt to justify what Ty had done.

"Well, why couldn't he be honest and let campus safety know then?" said Jamal.

"Don't worry I'm gon talk to him", said Kris.

"Whatever man", said Jamal.

Meanwhile, at his parents' house, his father broke the news to his mother and sister inside their four bedroom home. In utter shock belief, his mother doesn't know what to say. His father made sure that they all understood Jamal was actually innocent and was not selling drugs. He just got caught up with the wrong crowd.

"I always told him to stop being so naive, is he going to be expelled from school", asked Mrs Williams.

"Hopefully not", Mr Williams said.

Jamal went inside of the administration building to see if he could get excused for days he missed out of class.

"I'm here to get my days that I missed out of class excused," said Jamal to the front desk clerk.

"What's your reason and do you have anything in writing", she asked.

"Here you go Ms. Shaw", said Jamal as he handed her a copy of his arrest warrant. Soon as she read the document, she explained to him,

"Oh no sir, sorry we won't be able to excuse you for the fact of what took place".

"But those drugs that they found in my dorm room did not belonged to me, said Jamal.

"I'm sorry. I'm not the one to talk to about this", Ms Shaw said.

While in his classes, Jamal could hardly concentrate. It was difficult to not think about what had happened let alone remain attentive and receptive while being lectured in World Literature class. He went to visit his advisor, Dr Greggs.

"Oh Mr Williams, here to see me?" she asked.

"Yes, I need to talk to you".

"Good news?, asked Dr Greggs.

"No it's actually bad news," he said. They walked into her office and she shut the door.

"Well, what seems to be the problem, Jamal?" she asked.

"I got into some big trouble. Someone left drugs inside of my pillow and now I'm being blamed for it", Jamal explained.

Though in shock and disbelief, Dr Greggs held her composure. She asked him to wait patiently while she made a phone call.

She called her husband who's also a professor at Bazemore that teaches Political Science. Jamal sat and waited while she explained Jamal's situation. Once she ended the conversation with her husband, she said,

"It would be wise that you get a very good lawyer. "I'm just going to be honest with you. My husband said that the judicial system shows no favor, especially with African American men like yourself. So if I were you, I'd talk to my parents and see about investing in a good lawyer as soon as possible".

"Okay, Dr Greggs. I'll be sure to let them know".

As soon as Jamal left her office, he called his dad to let him know what his advisor told him.

When Jamal got back to his room, Craig said, "You too calm to not be active enough to handle this situation".

"What you mean?" Jamal asked.

"Look at you. I'd be in someone's office trying to get this resolved", Craig said.

"Easy for you to say", said Jamal.

"What you going to tell them?", asked Craig.

"No more than what I'm already doing", Jamal replied.

"You need to talk with President Simmons", Craig suggested.

"If I could get a hold of him", Jamal replied.

"If he's not in his office, check with one of the deans", said Craig.

Frustrated, Jamal decided to go back to the main campus to speak with someone. Luckily, he was able to meet with one of the deans, Dean Wilson. Jamal was polite and articulate, but little did Jamal knew that Dean Wilson was a heartless individual who could care less about Jamal's innocence.

"In my eyes, you got caught, you are guilty until proven innocent. You made the choice of allowing those gentlemen in your room. You have to face the consequences. You're a small fella Mr Williams, and you're gonna have a hard time getting those guys off of you in prison".

Jamal had no words and walked out of his office.

"Thanks for your help...brother", he said under his breath.

Jamal got back to his room.

"So how did it go?" asked Craig.

"Worse than what I thought", said Jamal. "All Dean Wilson did was condemn me and tell me how everything was my fault".

"At this point, just leave it to God", said Craig.

"At this point, I don't have a choice. He pretty much told me there's no hope for me at all. I'm not going to be able to deal with this. Either, I'm free of the charges and I don't have to deal with this or suspend me and let me start again next semester", said Jamal.

"If you have to leave, I'm moving out too. I don't trust anyone in this building anymore, especially Ty," said Craig.

Later, there was a knock on the door. Craig opened it and an officer from Campus Safety was there asking to speak with Jamal. He handed Jamal a letter in an envelope and asked for his signature on another form.

"Wow this is the cleanest male room dorm I've ever seen", said the officer.

"Yeah we keep it clean in here. But speaking of clean, you know I had to clean up all that mess yall made when yall searched the room the other night?" said Craig.

"Yeah sorry about that. We were just doing campus policy, said the officer as he left the room dancing to the music that was being played Jamal and Craig's dorm room.

Jamal opened the letter and it read:

> *Dear Mr Jamal Williams, you were recently charged with Possession of Marijuana with the intent to distribute on the campus of Bazemore College. Not only is this a crime in the city, county, and state level, but also the college campus code of law. In order to come up with a resolution for the crime committed which also classifies as a disciplinary act according to Bazemore College's Code of Ethics and Regulations, you are required to attend a mandatory hearing along with the college disciplinary board members. If you do not show up to this hearing, you will be automatically expelled. The hearing is scheduled for Monday, September 30th, at 8:30am.*

Jamal dropped the letter and lay down on the bed. He woke up later and took a walk outside. He noticed everyone as either smoking weed or carrying around alcohol. He was in utter disbelief at what he was witnessing. He was recently arrested because drugs were found inside his room, he was even charged, but no one was addressing the behavior that he saw.

"Hey you wanna hit this?" someone asked while passing him a blunt.

"Nah, I'm good", Jamal replied.

"What about a shot of this Henny?", again they asked.

Jamal just walked off and back into his dorm room. There he saw Craig, Ty and Kris smoking weed in his dorm room.

"Really? You got some nerve, said Jamal. Everyone else in the room were too high with a puzzled look on their face. "What's good with you Jamal," asked Kris.

"This is the reason I got locked up in the first place", said Jamal as he charges towards Ty. Kris and Craig tried to pull Jamal away from Ty, but he pushes them off and throws a punch into Ty's jaw. All of sudden, Jamal awakens out of his sleep. It was a dream. He looks towards Craig's bed and sees that he's asleep as well.

Chapter Six

THE HEARING

As Jamal awoke from his surreal dream, he said his prayers and left the room to go shower. Before he headed out, Craig wished him good luck. His father met up with him and they walked into the administration building where the hearing was being held. The administration building is one of the hugest and newer buildings on campus. They checked in and got on the elevator. Headed to room 400, Jamal's father got a chance to meet the rest of the guys who were in the room that night when Jamal was sent to the detention center, which were Ty, Kris, Bilal, JB, and Brooklyn. Jamal hopes to get redemption, but most importantly clarification on what his future looks like based on the incident that happened. The college disciplinary board members were present as well. These members were Bazemore College employees such as professors, deans, dorm directors, a member of the Student Government Association, and Mr Seawell. Mr Seawell who is the campus's IT supervisor in charge of resolving all of the campus's internet and computer maintenance issues. Mr Williams immediately recognized Mr Seawell. They both attended Bazemore around the same time. In fact, they were college classmates, but had different majors. Mr Williams walked towards Mr Seawell.

"Ronald Seawell, I haven't seen you in years. How you been", said Mr Williams in a whispering voice. Mr Seawell mirrored back by saying,

"Uh I've been great. It's great to see you also, but not on these unfortunate circumstances. I'll catch up with you after this is resolved"

Once they did a roll call, all of the gentlemen were asked to step out of the conference room and to wait patiently as they would call them back individually.

As the guys walked out, Bilal whispered to Jamal, "Is that your Pops?"

"Yeah," Jamal said.

"Is E mad at you?" Bilal asked.

"Nah, he cool", Jamal replied.

The first name they called was Ty's. Next was Kris, then Bilal, J.B., and Brooklyn. Jamal and his father were last. But while they were waiting, another student by the name of David was waiting on his hearing for an incident that occurred the same night Jamal and Brooklyn got arrested. Nervously sitting without being still, Mr Williams decided to have a conversation with him.

"So what you're in here for young man?" asked Mr Williams.

"I was in Donaldson Hall. As soon as I walked out, the officers accused me of pouring urine on this female from the top floor, simply because I'm from Florida", said the young man.

"What? That's ridiculous. What does you being from the state of Florida have to do with anything?", asked Mr Williams.

"I agree, but students from Florida here have a bad reputation. Just stupid—plain stupid—if you ask me," he said.

"Wow, I remember having class in Donaldson Hall", said Mr Williams to David.

"So, you're an alumni", asked David.

"Yep, class of 75, replied Mr Williams.

"Yo that's dope! The both of you attended the same HBCU! Like father, like son. The first time I ever seen something like this. I'm a first generation college student in my family" said David.

"When do you graduate", asked Mr Williams.

"In a few months actually. I'm a graduating senior", said David.

"Well, I wish you the best of luck", said Mr Williams.

As Brooklyn was leaving, he told Jamal and his father that he let the board know that Jamal didn't do anything and the drugs did not belong to him.

Jamal and his father entered the conference room as Jamal was called in last. They sat by each other as they listened to each member of the disciplinary board.

"We would like to make this clear that Bazemore College serves as a private institution, therefore this hearing doesn't have anything to do with anything you have to deal with so far as the county municipalities or the charge that you Jamal were charged with. Any questions", Mr Seawell, head of the disciplinary board asked.

"Yes, what happens if it's found that my son Jamal is guilty, which he is not, what happens then", asked Mr Williams.

"I spoke with Mr Williams prior, but I'll state this again. There's a program called PTI, which stands for Pre Trial Intervention. I've already made a recommendation that he gets accepted into the program. It will remove the charges off his record. He'll be good", said Officer Brooks.

"Just in case, if he doesn't gets accepted, then what, asked Mr Williams.

"There's no doubt. He will get in", said Officer Brooks.

"Okay, let's move on. Jamal tell us about yourself, said Mr Seawell.

They interrogated Jamal by asking him to explain what happened on the night of the incident.

"Well, I was walking to my dorm and ran into Kris. He told me about a get together they were having for Ty's birthday. They asked me to come through and so I did. Then we left to go to my dorm room. We were smoking weed and once we were done, we continued to just socialize. That's when Mr Phillips came to the room and contacted Public Safety", said Jamal.

They asked about his past, grades, and plans after graduation. "Any thing else you'd like to say Mr Jamal", asked Mr Seawell.

"Sure. There's a lot of things that happens on this campus and no one never faces the consequences, but now I'm being accused of drug possession with intent to distribute. Drugs that didn't belong to me by the way, but now I'm facing the blame. I don't want to be kicked out of school or sent to jail for something I didn't do.

"You'll be eligible for PTI. I'll make sure of that. You'll go through this program and you'll be able to get your record expunged. So don't worry about that, Jamal", said Officer Brooks.

"It will defeat my son's purpose of continuing his education here if he's convicted. This is his future. Is that a guarantee that he will get accepted into the program?" asked Jamal's father.

"Yes. I know the person in charge of that program," Officer Brooks replied.

"Anything you'd like to say, Mr Williams?" Mr Seawell asked Jamal's father.

"Yes, I just would like to say that our family has a legacy at this college and it would truly hurt me to see my son expelled from this institution. He does not belong back home. He needs his education. There's nothing to offer to a young black man in our hometown. He has never been in any type of trouble. So please, I'm asking you give him another chance", Jamal's father replied. Dr Dunn was in tears by hearing Jamal's side of the story and listening to his father as well. Learning that they both were Bazemore College men made him so emotional.

"This may sound weird, but I remember you when you were a student here", said Dr Dunn to Mr Williams.

"I remember you also", Mr Williams replied.

"One last question Mr Jamal. Why were you hanging with these gentlemen anyway? You seem so different from these guys", said Mr Seawell.

"I guess I was just trying to fit in", said Jamal.

The hearing meeting with Jamal and his dad came to a close. "You will receive a notification on our decision within one week. You will have two chances to appeal the decision, if it's an expulsion, said Mr Seawell".

Eventually, Jamal and his dad exited from the meeting and headed out of the administration building. They took a walk around the campus and his father noticed how much the college campus changed since his undergrad days.

"Wow, things have sure gotten wilder here", he said.

"What do you mean, Dad?" Jamal asked.

"You got women walking around here disrespecting their bodies, guys cussing and carrying on. My, has the generation has gotten worse", said Mr Williams.

"I made a huge mistake by allowing those guys to come in my dorm room," said Jamal.

"Well, don't beat yourself up about it. We are going to get through this once and for all", said Mr Williams.

"I truly hope so."

Jamal and his father went for lunch, then his father returned back to work.

Chapter Seven

TO APPEAL

Hoping everything was back to normal, Jamal was to be in a better mood. Although everyone around him was still smoking weed, Jamal felt he needed to be focused on his situation instead. So, he tried to avoid them, but it was difficult since drugs and alcohol on the campus of Bazemore College was such a normal activity.

While leaving from campus to visit a relative, Jamal bumped into the dorm director, Mr Phillips.

"Hey did anyone confess?", Mr Phillips asked.

"No, I don't think so, Mr Phillips," Jamal replied.

"That's not good", said Mr Phillips.

Jamal was in a rush to leave campus to get away from all the stress and anxiety. It was definitely hard for him to focus in class so this little weekend getaway was definitely something he needed.

After the weekend, Jamal was on his way back to his dorm when Mr Phillips walked up to him immediately.

"Here's your letter from the board, Williams," he said.

Jamal opened up the letter and saw that the college had decided to put him on disciplinary suspension. However, he did have the opportunity to appeal. He immediately went to the library to begin writing a letter to appeal the board's decision. Once he finished writing his letter, he went to the writing lab to get some assistance in critiquing and editing his letter. Amazed by his writing skills and unhappy with the incident that occurred, Ms Coker, the writing lab supervisor, said; "It's a shame what happened. So sorry that it had to happen to you".

She constantly complimented Jamal on his writing. However, he was only focused on getting his letter completed at the moment. She edited his letter and Jamal went back to make further corrections.

"You're good at writing, I see. Maybe you should consider being a writer one day. This would make a good story", said Ms Coker.

"Whatever, lady," Jamal said to himself.

Two days later, Jamal got another letter from the board and their decision to suspend him for the semester remained. The only difference this time was they dropped the fine charge for smoking inside the building. Initially, Jamal was charged with a fine of $100. He ended up back to the writing lab to get more help to appeal once more.

Another hectic week. "I'll be glad when this is all over", Jamal said to himself.

Jamal decided to take another weekend getaway. This time he hitched a ride with a friend, Donovan, to his hometown. There, he met up with several of his friends outside of college and broke down the news about what happened to him at school.

"That's messed up Jamal", said Donovan. "You sure you don't want me to come on campus and handle that for you?" Donovan asked.

Jamal knew it was over and it didn't matter what Donovan could do for him, other than finding a lawyer. He still had a real court date hearing. School was beginning to be stressful. He didn't mind having a break.

At this moment, Jamal was interested in being around friends from his hometown. Since Donovan lived in the same city where Bazemore College is located, he told Jamal that if he got suspended, he could always crash at his place free of charge.

Jamal just wanted to have fun and get his mind off the situation so he gathered his friends for a night out. Inside the club, everyone was either smoking or drinking. Donovan began to smoke a blunt with Jamal. At first, he hesitated, but Jamal went on to smoke.

The next morning he had a hangover and woke up to a phone call from Mr Phillips. Jamal answered anxiously to find out what he wanted. Unfortunately, the college had made its final decision and Jamal was told he needed to move out of his dorm room immediately. Jamal was devastated by the news, but also felt relieved that he wouldn't have to worry about classes anymore. He could just focus on his actual court hearing. He was only suspended for the remainder of the semester. Once he came back for the next semester, he would be placed on disciplinary probation.

Chapter Eight

SUSPENDED FROM COLLEGE

Jamal and his father had a talk as Jamal prepared to take his father's car back to school to move all of his belongings out of the dorm room. They discussed what Jamal's plans will be while he'll be out of school the next few months.

"Well, I could stay at Donovan's apartment. It's not that far from campus", said Jamal. "Donovan Montgomery" his father asked.

"Yes", Jamal replied.

"Wow, that's great to hear. I always thought that kid would end up in jail somewhere", his father stated.

Donovan had sort of a bad history of trouble, but lately he'd been able to stay out of trouble. His father trusted his decision, but reminded him it was only temporary.

"Next semester you're going back to school. Just let this time away be a time of regrouping and concentrating on bettering your future so don't get comfortable", said Mr Williams.

Jamal headed to his dormitory and began moving all of his belongings out. He also had to withdraw from the college as well, which meant he had to fill out a withdrawal form and get signatures from each department chair. One department chair in particular, Dr. Miriam Lunsford, was heartbroken when she learned what happened to Jamal.

"Oh my, you don't seem like a bad person at all. Do you mind if I asked what happened?" Dr Lunsford asked.

"Well, to make a long story short, I allowed some certain people in my dorm room, one thing led to the next, and all of a sudden I'm blamed for something I had little control over, simply because no one confessed to it", Jamal explained.

"I can tell you're a good person. Is there anything that I can do?" asked Dr Lunsford.

"You can talk to anyone, including the president, that there needs to be a better job done in the college's judicial system. Also, one last thing you can do for me is pray for me", said Jamal.

"I will most definitely, young man. I want to see you back here next semester too", said Dr Lunsford.

"Thanks, I will", said Jamal as he walked out of her office and left off campus.

Jamal made one last visit to Donovan's apartment. He lets him know of the school's decision and that he needed a place to crash ASAP. Donovan lived within minutes of Bazemore campus. He explained the situation to him.

"I'm going to have to look for a job. I only have like $250 in my savings".

"Stop it. Don't worry about nothing. I got you", said Donovan.

"Well I got to get back home and have my pops drop me back here", Jamal said. "Screw all that, I gotta go down there anyway. So I'll come and get you and bring you back", Donovan said.

So it all worked out for Jamal. He was suspended from school, but was able to live temporarily with Donovan, which meant he was still not too far from the Bazemore College campus. If he ever wanted to still eat in the caf, he still had his ID card as they accidentally forgot to revoke it. Although, if caught on campus by any official who recognized his face, he could end up with another charge for trespassing.

Donovan finally picked up Jamal later that evening at Jamal's parents house.

"Don't worry Mr and Mrs Williams, he's in safe hands and he'll be back in school next semester", said Donovan to Jamal's parents.

They had a long but great discussion regarding Jamal.

"So why you came down anyway?" asked Jamal on their way back.

"Had some business I needed to take care of. Plus I needed to see my fam", Donovan replied.

Jamal called Kris and let him know he'd still not be too far from campus at Donovan's apartment.

Chapter Nine

A FREE VACATION AT DONOVAN'S PLACE

ONCE JAMAL AND DONOVAN ARRIVED at Donovan's apartment, there were already people there waiting for Donovan to bring back some product so he can make his profit. It appeared that Donovan was a drug dealer. That's why he made several frequent visits to their hometown so he could run drug transactions. He also constantly wore a work uniform.

"So what is it that you do?" asked Jamal, giving Donovan the benefit of the doubt.

"I'm a working man. You see me in a work uniform don't you?" he asked Jamal.

Jamal nods his head, yes.

"Well, that's all you need to know, especially if you're going to be paranoid", said Donovan with a smirk on his face.

Another surprise that Jamal was not aware of, was Donovan also had other roommates who crash from time to time. Some nights, they would have parties that lasted several hours into the night. This was no problem for Jamal. The time he spent there was just to be away from home as he waited to re-enter school the next upcoming semester.

Jamal didn't want to be a bum or freeload and become unproductive, so a few days later, he decided to go looking for a job. After several weeks of job hunting, he had no luck. Donovan explained to Jamal that he didn't have to contribute to the rent.

During this time at Donovan's, Jamal encountered a lot of people with many different personalities.

One morning, Donovan left really early to handle some so-called business.

"If anyone comes knocking on the door who you don't recognize, text me first, then find out what they want", he said to Jamal.

"Okay", relied Jamal.

Several people knocked on the door at Donovan's apartment looking for him. Each time Jamal texted or called Donovan, he'd get no response. There was one guy in particular who stopped by. When Jamal texted Donovan, he received a response. Donovan calls Jamal.

"Don't worry. That's my boy Mike. He works at the Plaza Hotel Downtown. Ask how much he need", said Donovan.

"Donovan wants to know how much you need", Jamal asked Mike.

"Yo tell him I need about 3 oz, because I got Young B waiting at the hotel", said Mike. Jamal relayed the message.

"Tell him to sit tight and I'll be there in a few", said Donovan.

"He said he's coming", said Jamal.

"Where's he performing", Jamal asked Mike in disbelief.

"At Bazemore homecoming", Mike replied.

"That's where I attend school", said Jamal.

"Oh yeah, why you not in class?", asked Mike.

"Long story, but I'll be back next semester", said Jamal.

Mike left and told Jamal to let Donovan know he'll be on standby to see him later.

As weeks passed by, Jamal still couldn't get any luck with a job. At least he had a special savings account that helped him out tremendously with finances. There were certain points of depression for Jamal. What helped him was meeting the various people who would come to Donovan's apartment as well as writing in a journal. He wrote poetry, rap lyrics, and was even inspired to begin writing a movie script based on what happened to him at school.

It was time for his court date and both of his parents came to pick him up at Donovan's apartment. They arrived for the court appearance, but were told that his court case had been rescheduled. It appeared that no Public Defender was assigned to Jamal nor Brooklyn's case. During this time also, workers from the Clerk of Court Office informed Jamal once more of the PTI program. This was the same program that Officer Brooks kept stressing when the initial incident occurred at school. This program would include community service and counselling that would prevent Jamal from having a criminal record. One of the workers from the Clerk of Court's office referred Jamal to the PTI office. As they walked out of her office, they realized she was a Bazemore College graduate as well. Her diploma hung inside her office.

They met with the advisors for the PTI program. After Jamal explained everything to the advisor, she said, "Be honest. Are you learning anything at Bazemore?"

Jamal replied, "Why yes, I am," in a very serious voice.

"Wow, that's the first time I've ever heard that. A lot of students from Bazemore come here for court. I understand that school has a negative reputation", she said.

"Well, I'm a graduate from there", said Jamal's father. "Bazemore College is what you make it", said Jamal.

She apologized and began to lecture Jamal about the program as well as the consequences if he did not enroll into the program. "Hopefully this is a wake up call for you, because you're at a very vulnerable stage in your life. You don't want to get trapped and caught up in this system that is designed to keep many young African American men like yourself down", said the advisor.

The more she talked about the possibilities of Jamal ending up in jail, the more teary eyed both of his parents got. The cost for the program was $200 which Jamal's father had no hesitation in paying. He quickly walked out of the office to find the nearest ATM to get cash to pay for the program. The payment was non-refundable.

Jamal's parents finally got a chance to meet Brooklyn's mother as well. They took a plane all the way from New York to attend the court hearing.

"So you travelled all the way from New York?" asked Jamal's father.

"Yes. This whole senseless act has been a nightmare. Not only has it affected my son, but our family too", said Brooklyn's mother, Ms Nunez. She explained that Brooklyn has never gotten into any trouble ever like this and he was an "A" student. Jamal's father also spoke of his clean record and non criminal history.

"Well thank God for this PTI Program", said Jamal's father to Brooklyn's mother.

"Yes, thank God, but unfortunately my son won't be coming back down south to attend Bazemore College", stated Brooklyn's mother.

After spending hours at court, Jamal's big day was finally over resulting in another court date with the expectation of getting accepted into the PTI program. Feeling confident, Jamal told Donovan the good news. They decided to celebrate by taking shots of vodka and bourbon. There were also blunts of weed rolled and smoked in heavy rotation, but Jamal made sure to stay away from it. He did not want to ruin any chances of getting enrolled into the PIT program. It was understood that part of this program included urine tests for drugs.

Chapter Ten

THE SECOND COURT VISIT

As a few more weeks passed, the semester which Jamal missed the latter half of, it was time for the next court date appearance. This time, Jamal's mother decided not to go and have just his father go instead. They were already anticipating to start the PTI program after this appearance. Jamal and his co-defendant were expected to arrive at 8 am. So they did, but still no public defenders were present. Jamal was getting a little worried. He thought he would have to represent himself, but then he thought, why would he need a lawyer anyway if he's going to enroll into the PTI program? His charge would be dismissed.

All of the defendants had to wait on their names to be called. As Jamal and Brooklyn were waiting, a 16 year old African American kid was crying to his public defender. "I don't want to go to jail" he said.

The judge called Jamal's name and asked how he wished to plead. Jamal felt that a plea would be unnecessary, he told the judge that he signed up for PTI.

"You have been disqualified from participating in the PTI program", said the solicitor, a tall Caucasian man with dark hair who wouldn't look at Jamal at all. "How do you wish to plead?", he asked Jamal again.

Since Jamal didn't know what to say, he just stated that he wish to plead the trial.

The judge asked, "Are you serious young man?" and chuckled. "Have you spoken to your lawyer yet?" he asked in a thick southern accent.

"No," Jamal said.

"I think you need to speak with your lawyer first, because if you plead a trial with a charge like this, there's no doubt you're going to do some time. Come back at 4:30 after you talk with your lawyer. Next," said the judge.

The same went for Brooklyn. They both had different lawyers, but Brooklyn didn't apply for PTI since he was going to transfer his case back to New York. Jamal's father realized that he did not get into the PTI program and was in a state of mixed emotions - he felt betrayed by the system.

"Why didn't you get into the program?", asked Jamal's dad.

"I don't know, the judge said I need to speak to my lawyer first", replied Jamal.

"Well, who's your lawyer?", said Mr Williams.

"They said his name is Carl Johnson", said Jamal.

As Jamal and his father were walking out of the courtroom they noticed Jamal's public defender with the name tag "Carl Johnson". Jamal approached him and introduced himself. Attorney Johnson had his file and immediately said he should apply for PTI.

"He was told that he was denied", said Jamal's dad.

"Wait one sec while I look into this", said the attorney.

Jamal and his dad sat down and waited as they tried to figure out why Jamal would be denied from PTI.

"Why would they deny me?", asked Jamal. "Hopefully it's just a mistake".

"Besides, I paid $200 for the enrollment fee", said his dad.

Attorney Johnson came back and explained why Jamal was denied. "It has something to do with the negative reputation of Bazemore College. Being that the school is private gives them their own jurisdiction, therefore officers are welcome to give offenders a slap on the wrist. Evidently, this is one of those rare situations where the officers at your school arrested you for a non-violent crime", said the attorney. "It seems like to me you were made out as an example to warn any other students at Bazemore".

All Jamal could do was shake his head while looking down.

"Why did those people lie to me and make you think you were going to be accepted in the PTI program?", said Jamal's father.

"That's how they make their money. See, if you plea guilty, the judge will give you at least one year of probation since this is your first and only crime. Not to mention, you're a college student", said Attorney Johnson.

"What are the odds", asked Mr Williams.

"Will this prevent him from receiving financial aid for school", asked Jamal's dad.

"Yes, I'm afraid so", said the attorney.

Jamal and his dad left to get something to eat. All they could do was discuss the situation of being in court and getting back into school for the next semester. By now, it was time for Jamal to report back to court, he was confident and ready to get it over with. The judge called him and Brooklyn up to the front of the court.

"How do you wish to plead", asked the judge.

"Your honor, my client would like to plead guilty, but before doing so, could the solicitor explain again why my client was denied PTI", said Jamal's Public Defender.

The judge allowed the solicitor to respond. "He was denied because the incident happened on the campus of a private college, in which this same college has a known history of not properly punishing their students as they should. Therefore we requested that he gets at least one year probation, where he has to complete a drug counseling class, and 40 hours of community service", said the solicitor.

"Is this agreed upon", asked the judge.

"Yes your honor", said Attorney Johnson.

The judge asked if Jamal had any words he'd like to say. Jamal stepped up the microphone.

"First of all I'd like to say that I was never a drug dealer, just at the wrong place at the wrong time. My intentions are to just get an education and graduate. I appreciate your decision of not sending me to prison, thank you", said Jamal.

Once it was final, both young men were finally at ease, although Jamal was on probation, while Brooklyn was in the process of getting his case transferred back to New York. They took Jamal's driver's license since it would be suspended for the next six months. Jamal was told that his probation would start immediately and would need to get registered for community service as well as drug counseling.

Jamal and Brooklyn said their final farewells to each other. They gave each other a hug and a dap.

"I won't be coming back to Bazemore next semester," said Brooklyn.

"You're going to transfer to another college?", asked Jamal.

"I'm going back to community college to get my associates'. I may even go to Job Corps and pick up a trade," said Brooklyn.

Brooklyn's mother walked up to Jamal. "I just have one question for you young man," as she asked in her Jamaican accent.

"Yes mam," said Jamal.

"Why did you allow all those guys in your room in the first place?" she asked.

"I just wasn't thinking," said Jamal.

"Be mindful of the company you keep," Brooklyn's mom said.

The court session ended. Jamal's probation started. Since Brooklyn was a resident of New York, his case was transferred.

Jamal and his father headed back to Donovan's apartment to get his belongings. On the way back home, Jamal had a minor breakdown. Reality struck him as he thought about how the court's decision would affect his future. Now that he was home just in time for Christmas break, many of his other friends from college were home also. Every now and then Donovan would even show up, but Jamal tried to stay away to avoid issues with the law. He couldn't afford to get arrested again.

Chapter Eleven

THE NEXT SEMESTER

JAMAL'S FATHER DROVE HIM BACK to school for the new semester. As they arrived on campus, Jamal was excited and motivated. He went to housing registration to request his dorm room key, but was told to go to the Admissions department first to re-enroll.

"I have to reapply," Jamal explained to his father. So they went to the Admissions building. Jamal explained the situation to the clerk.

"Fill this out Mr Williams," said the clerk as she handed him an application on a clipboard.

Once Jamal completed and returned it to the admissions clerk, he was cleared and eligible for a dorm room key. He registered for a room through housing registration where he was told that his room assignment was back at the Hazelwood Street dormitory.

Jamal and his father moved his things back into his new dorm room. He checked in and met with Mr Phillips.

"Welcome back Mr Williams. Great to have you back", said Mr Phillips.

"Why thank you Mr Phillips. It is also great to have you as a dorm director again," said Jamal in a disguised sarcastic tone. Jamal felt resentful over the fact that Mr Phillips had total control of the incident from last semester and should've used better judgment or at least issued a verbal warning instead of calling campus officials. But Mr Phillips and the public safety officers who arrested him were only doing their job.

After Jamal finished arranging his things in his dorm room, he and his father ate dinner at a buffet restaurant close by.

"So how you feel about returning to school this semester?" his father asked.

"I'm happy and proud, because this gives me an opportunity to prove my true character to Bazemore despite the odds that will be against me. I have to do community service, attend drug counseling, and meet with my probation officer. Not to mention, I have to take 18 credit hours for school," said Jamal. "So I have a lot on my plate this year."

"You can do it," said his father.

They returned to campus, then Jamal's father headed back home.

"Study hard," his father said as he left. Jamal went back to his room and started unpacking. His room door opened and his new roommate came in.

"What's up, I'm Earl, but everyone calls me Live," he said.

"I'm Jamal," said Jamal.

"I see we don't have a fridge. Guess I'll come back and bring mine," said Earl as he scoped out the room. "I'm on the football team, so you probably won't see me as much. I'm usually up the street at the SCU at my girl's apartment," he explained.

He exited out of the room and tells Jamal,

"I'll be back in a couple of days with my fridge from home".

Later that evening, Jamal reunited with some of his old buddies from last semester. One guy named Herbert asked Jamal, "Can you please explain what happened last semester?"

"We were all smoking in my room. I didn't know anyone had weed on them, let alone...", said Jamal as Herb interrupted him.

Herb stood up and asked Jamal, "You know who did it?"

"Yeah, you know Ty?" said Jamal.

"So, how would like to handle this? What do you want to do?" asked Herb.

They walked around campus until they bumped into Kris. They exchanged daps.

"So where's Ty?" asked Herb.

"He's not coming back," said Kris.

"Why not?" asked Jamal.

"His parents not letting him," Kris explained.

"Well, do his parents even know how he left weed in my pillow and didn't claim it causing me to go to jail for a felony charge that I can't get off my record?" asked Jamal.

"Wait, what?" asked Kris.

"I was charged with a felony, which is going to follow me for the rest of my life. It could've been easily avoided by the way," explained Jamal.

Next, he saw his former roommate, Craig.

"What's up Craig?" Jamal said.

"I moved off campus. It was so messed up after what happened, I decided to move off campus," said Craig.

"This is the exact reason why I stay to myself a lot and keep myself busy working my little part time job", he added.

Chapter Twelve

PROBATION: THE FIRST HALF

JAMAL HAD A FULL DAY ahead of him. He completed his class registration. Then he ran into Officer Brooks.

"Well, well, well. Mr Jamal, how are you?" he asked.

"I'm ok," said Jamal.

"I don't get a thank you?" said Officer Brooks.

Jamal asks, "Thank you for what?".

"Didn't you get PTI so that charge doesn't stay on your record?" asked Officer Brooks.

"No, in fact I was denied PTI, because Bazemore College is a private school with its own jurisdiction that has a bad reputation for criminal activities amongst the students, so they denied my application," explained Jamal.

Officer Brooks walked off speechless and surprised at the same time, saying, "I'll get back with you on that."

Luckily, Jamal's probation officer's office was located within walking distance from the Bazemore campus. Jamal doesn't have a car, but again, his license is suspended. met his probation officer, named Officer Wilson, for the very first time.

"Here's my ground rules: Don't ever fail a pee test, pay your fees on time, and always show up when it's time to meet with me. You do those things, we'll get along just fine," said Officer Wilson.

He also gave Jamal his community service work orders as well as his drug counseling session requirements.

"I also do surprise visits for some of my probationers. Matter of fact, you're not the only Bazemore student that's been assigned to me," said Officer Wilson.

After leaving his meeting with his probation officer, Jamal had to meet with the drug counseling service agency. There, he met with Lisa to discuss the purpose of the program. Lisa was one the head persons to help him along the way in the drug counseling program.

"The only reason I'm here is because of my probation. I do not have a drug problem. Just was hanging with the wrong crowd", said Jamal. With attending drug counseling sessions, completing community service hours, meeting with his probation officer once a month, and taking 18 credit hours for school, Jamal had a lot on his plate this semester. He wouldn't have time for social activities or even a part-time job.

As the semester started, Jamal attended his probationary duties to attend drug counseling and community service. Jamal was required to complete eight sessions of drug counseling and 40 hours of community service, which consisted of eight hours per day. Jamal chose to get the requirements out of the way without missing or showing up late every week that he attended.

During community service, he met all kinds of personalities. Most of the offenders seemed like they would continue being criminals. Especially the teenagers. They continued to recognize themselves as gang members. Others talked a lot about their current drug use.

One guy named Antwan, who was arrested for a simple possession charge of marijuana, asked Jamal what brought him to do community service.

"I got caught up with the wrong crowd," said Jamal.

"What you mean", asked Antwan.

"Let's just say I got arrested for PWID for some weed that didn't belong to me," said Jamal.

The guy shook his head and said, "No way. You're a better man than me. You should've applied for PTI."

"I did, but they denied me," said Jamal.

"Why is that?" he asked.

"Because it happened on Bazemore campus within their own jurisdiction," said Jamal.

"Wow, they really screwed you over man," said the guy.

"Yeah the people from PTI just took my parents money; it was non-refundable," said Jamal.

"I'm not talking about them," he said.

"Who, my public defender, the solicitor?" asked Jamal.

"They screwed you over too, but I'm still not talking about him either," he said. "I'm talking about Bazemore College. Just think about it," said Antwan.

"I can bet you they asked you who it belonged to and you said you didn't know right", asked Antwan.

"At the time I really didn't know," said Jamal.

"Doesn't matter. The first person that squeal gets the deal," he said with a smirk on his face.

"What does that mean?" asked Jamal.

"That's why it's also good to watch cop shows," he pointed out.

"They knew those drugs didn't belonged to you. They were just waiting for you to say it was one of the other guys. You were the only one who got arrested too, right?" asked Antwan.

"No, I had a co-defendant who was also with me. They found weed on him as well," said Jamal.

"The reason why they didn't kick you out out of school completely, because your student loans is their profit", said Antwan. It made a lot of sense to Jamal. Jamal went on to tell him that his co-defendant Brooklyn transferred his case back to his home state of New York.

"He's lucky, because more than likely they're going to throw his case out. They're a little more lenient towards weed charges up North," he said. "You should've just said it was one of the guys'. Sooner or later, one of them would've confessed to it."

He suggested that Jamal apply for a pardon. "You'll still have a record, but at least you'll be able to have most of your civil rights back, except getting a federal government job or applying for a clearance.

Jamal was devastated.

The next week, Jamal had his official meeting for his drug counseling sessions. He sat in a room with a group of others. There, he witnessed many others whom had other problems. One guy was an engineer who got a DUI in Los Angeles, California while on a business trip for his job. Jamal could tell he didn't wanted to be there. The next time Jamal attended his drug counseling session meetings, he met Khalil, another student at Bazemore.

"So let me guess, you were one of the athletes that almost got busted last year" asked Jamal.

Nothing I'm proud of but yeah. Thank God Bazemore still gave me another chance", said Khalil.

"I committed the exact same offense," Jamal told him.

After the session, Jamal asked Khalil about his drug charge.

"They just charged me with simple possession and I was able to get out on a PR bond. I'm working on getting the charge expunged now", said Khalil.

"Wow, I've been totally screwed, said Jamal.

"What happened with your charge?" Khalil asked.

"Well, I allowed some guys in my room to smoke weed, which I'm guilty of, but what I wasn't aware of was that someone hid weed in my pillow. Not just a little bag, I'm talking a half ounce with three small individual bags. No PR Bond, no PTI, therefore I have a felony that cannot be expunged off my record", said Jamal.

"Whoa, that's heavy", said Khalil as they both walked back on campus.

Meanwhile, Jamal also hustles to complete his community service hours once a week. He worked every Saturday for five weeks and completed his drug counseling sessions in eight weeks. He was very diligent and determined of getting these things done. He understood how important it was to stay out of trouble and having freedom. During his last drug counseling session, Khalil did not show. However, there was a former attendee was was sent back to repeat the program again.

"Randy, is that you?" said Lisa.

"Yes mam, it's me", he responded.

Randy, who was a college dropout had almost completed the program. Once you complete eight sessions, two weeks later you have to come back for a final urinary drug testing. This was a requirement. Randy didn't pass his last and final drug test for the program.

"I was very close in completing the program, but I gave in the night before and smoked a joint of bud", said Randy. He gave Jamal some words of encouragement, "Don't make the same mistake I made, be strong, because it isn't worth it", he said.

After leaving his final session, Jamal felt really relieved. Although, he still had one last drug test to take in two weeks to finally complete the drug counseling program, it felt a lot better that he was making good progress within his probation. Also, Jamal was doing well in school. Two weeks had passed and Jamal was prepared for his exit from the program. He passed his final drug test, but still had to take his monthly drug testing for his probation officer visits.

At his next meeting with his probation officer, Officer Wilson had to verify if Jamal completed his requirements first. Once he verified that Jamal was done with community service hours and drug counseling, he explained that he just needed to pay his restitution fees and continue to successfully pass his mandatory drug tests. "See you next month," said Officer Wilson.

Jamal walked out with confidence knowing this probation would not tear him down, but build him back up instead.

As the semester ended, Jamal passed all of his courses. His GPA was 3.23. It was a well-deserved result because he had put in a lot of work for Jamal's sake. Most of Jamal's classmates were sticking around for summer school and working part-time jobs. Since Jamal didn't have a car, he decided to go back home and work to save up enough to buy and get himself a car as soon as his six-month driver license suspension was over.

He was able to work a job at a summer youth camp. This job came in handy for him, since there weren't any background checks involved in order to get hired. There he met several other college students who were also in need of a summer job also. All of the other student workers attended prestigious universities, which made Jamal feel inferior, like an outsider. Not only did he attend a college with a bad reputation, but also was also a victim of being arrested at the school he attends.

Davis, a genius with a 4.0 GPA, asked Jamal, "So is it true you have to duck from bullets at Bazemore?"

"No, but is it true you have to duck from pedophiles at SCU?" asked Jamal sarcastically.

All the workers giggled.

"It was a joke," said Davis.

"And mines wasn't?" asked Jamal.

By the time Jamal worked enough to save up for a car, he made his first visit to his probation officer during summer break. At first, Jamal did not feel like driving to go see his probation officer. In fact, he thought about not showing up. Eventually, he snapped out of negative thought and decided to go see him. This caused him to rush, but he was able to make it. Unfortunately, he was thirty minutes late. Because of his tardiness, his probation officer automatically assigned Jamal for more community service hours, but then he had a change of heart.

"You know what, today has been a good day so far. I'm going to let this slide since you've been doing really good. I've never had a problem out of you," said Officer Wilson.

"Thank you so much," said Jamal.

"All of your restitution fees have been paid and you've met all of your requirements. Your next visit will be every three months from now on," said Officer Wilson.

As Jamal was heading his way back home, he noticed a flashing light in his rearview mirror. It was a cop car. Jamal thought to himself if he was speeding? He attempted to slow down, but the cop car switched lanes and drove ahead of Jamal. What a relief, he thought to himself, especially with the good news from his probation officer as well as his progress being on probation.

Chapter Thirteen
PROBATION: THE FINAL HALF

The new semester started. Jamal's parents helped him top-up the money he had saved to buy his very first car, a 1996 burgundy Mazda pickup. He travelled back to college and headed for registration. This time he moved into a suite with one roommate and two other suitemates. Jamal realized that since he had a vehicle, he needed to find a part-time job to properly maintain it. So he applied to several of the fast food burger places in the area.

One restaurant in particular was interested in hiring Jamal. He got a call back and spoke with one of the managers. Jamal was very excited to know that he would have the possibility of a part-time job while in school. Just the thought of it appealed to him. Not only was he excited about the money, but having something to do while in college would be welcome as well.

He met with one of the managers as they went over his application. They also discussed his school schedule.

"Have you ever been convicted of a felony?" the manager asked, but Jamal originally answered "No."

"Are you sure you don't have anything on your record?" asked the manager.

"The reason why I'm asking is because we just had a young man who we recently declined all because he lied on his application", she went on to add.

"Okay, I confess. I do have something on my record", admitted Jamal.

"No problem. I don't need to know what it is. You're going to have to go down to the police station and get a copy of your arrest record. We'll need that copy please sir, if you don't mind," said the manager.

After Jamal left, he went directly to the nearest police station. He walked inside. The cost for a copy of his arrest record was $25. He paid for it and was able to retrieve the copy. At his next meeting with the hiring manager, he presented the arrest record to her. She took his social security card and driver's license ID. She even gave him a schedule of which days he'd be working. She told him that he was hired upon the general manager's approval.

"Don't worry, you'll get it," she told Jamal.

Jamal was happy.

The very next day, the same manager called Jamal. She told him that the general manager did not approve of his application because of the charge on his record.

"Why?" Jamal asked.

"Since your charge is equivalent to a cocaine charge and it's pretty recent, we won't be able to hire you," she said. The manager felt bad having to tell Jamal the bad news. "I wish there was something I could do," she said. She referred him to some other places that didn't do background checks.

If he couldn't get a job at a burger joint, where could he get a job? Jamal thought about this for a very long time.

The very next job he applied for was a server at a soul food buffet restaurant. However, this time Jamal decided to take his chances and lie about his felony conviction. Luckily, he still managed to get hired. He discovered there were many other Bazemore College students employed there as well.

About three weeks had passed and Jamal was satisfied with the extra money that he was making while in school. He called his new job to find out what was his schedule for the current week.

"Jamal, is there something you're not telling us? We got a red flag from your application about your background check," said the general manager.

"I'm going to be honest. I have a criminal history".

"You lied on the application, therefore you're not eligible to work here anymore. I'm sorry, there's nothing else I can do. You should've just told the truth. This is from corporate, not me. Everyone makes mistakes," said the general manager.

"Before applying here, I tried to get a job at a fast food place and they wouldn't hire me because of my record. I felt like I had no choice," said Jamal.

"Well, again this is coming from corporate. I have nothing to do with this anymore," said the general manager. A week later, Jamal returned to get his final paycheck.

Another semester was coming to an end, and Jamal had his final meeting with his probation officer. He took his final urine test for drug use, which he passed. Officer Wilson went over all of his requirements he met for probation. Officer Wilson also told him that he still had another year to not be involved in any other infractions with the law.

"Everything looks good. Congratulations on successfully completing probation. I wish you nothing but the best of luck," he said.

"Thanks," said Jamal.

Jamal walked out of Officer Wilson's office at the state parole, probation, and pardon building as a happy man.

The last day to move out of the dorms was closely arriving. Jamal was about to enter his dorm room. A student by the name of Jimmy asked him for a favor as they both were the only two standing in the hallway. He wanted Jamal to take him to a bookstore across town to get more money for his books on SCU campus. Jamal noticed something weird about Jimmy, but couldn't lay a finger on it. Being a helpful Samaritan, Jamal agreed and drove him to the bookstore.

When Jamal got back to his dorm room, his suitemates informed him that their PlayStation 2 was missing.

"Did you let anyone inside here?" asked one of the suitemates.

"Nah, the only person I can remember was Jimmy, but he never came inside," said Jamal.

Mr Phillips, the dorm director arrived and started his investigation. Although, this time Jamal wasn't in any trouble, it felt a little traumatic as it reminded him about the incident that happened the previous year. Mr Phillips began to ask questions.

"Where were you before you came to your room", Mr Phillips asked Derwin, who was one of Jamal's suitemate.

"We all were at the Caf", said Derwin. They all except Jamal were at the Caf. The Caf is short for cafeteria.

"Mr Williams, where were you", asked Mr Phillips.

"I was off campus, but when I came back on the hallway towards the dorm room, I ran into Jimmy and gave him a ride to the bookstore on SCU campus".

"Did you notice anything suspicious about him", asked Mr Phillips.

"You know what? Come to think about it, he was acting a little strange", said Jamal.

"Well did you see him took the PlayStation", Mr Phillips asked.

"No, but he had a backpack", Jamal stated.

One of the suitemates had some issues with his room key. Therefore, the door stayed opened until any of the other suitemates were able to come and lock it. Jamal just discovered this. Mr Phillips and a campus security officer left the guys room. The other suitemates were a little suspicious of Jamal thinking he had something to do with this.

Mr Phillips came back with the Sony PlayStation and Jamal suitemates were relieved. "You're going to have to walk to campus safety headquarters to let the officers know if you would like to press charges or not," said Mr Phillips.

Jimmy was handcuffed and escorted.

"Should we press charges on him" said Rick, who was Jamal's roommate.

"Yeah", they all said at the same time.

When they got to the headquarters, it instantly brought back unpleasant memories for Jamal.

"Before you guys decide to press any charges, I just would like you all to know that if Jimmy is taken to booking, there's a possibility he'll be there till the New Years, because the judge is going on vacation" said one of the officers.

"Fellas I'm sorry. This was a huge mistake. Please don't press charges. I can't miss Christmas. My daughter's birthday is on Christmas," pleaded Jimmy.

Jamal thought to himself that he didn't had it as bad when he was arrested. In fact, He stayed less than 24 hours when he went to jail. They could see the fear that was in Jimmy's eyes.

"Why did you steal from our room?" asked Derwin, whom the PlayStation belonged to. Derwin was very upset and was ready to press charges on Jimmy.

"I was just looking for a ride from someone to take me to the bookstore. I didn't know the door was unlocked until I just so happen to try opening the door. I saw the PlayStation and I just allowed the devil to take over my judgment. I'm sorry guys," said Jimmy.

"So by the time I saw you, you had already taken the PlayStation?" asked Jamal.

Officer Brooks stepped into the room. "What's going on here?" he asked.

"This young man entered their dorm room and stole their PlayStation", said the other officer.

Officer Brooks was eager to take someone to jail. It was almost like he would get a special raise or promotion.

"If I were you guys I'd press charges on him and let him sit in jail," said Officer Brooks. The officers allowed Jamal and his roommates to discuss among themselves of how they should handle the situation.

"Hey it wasn't my playstation, so whatever decision you make Derwin, I'm still with you. I just feel like I been used against you and I didn't know he was going to do this", said Jamal.

"It wasn't your fault Jamal, but no lie, I would like to press charges on him", said Derwin.

"Fellas, let's just try to think this through. Jimmy's a young black college student like all of us. You got your Playstation back Derwin. Let him go and allow God to deal with him. Besides, I can't stand that punk cop Officer Brooks guy anyway. He's just another hateful cop waiting to lock up his own kind anyway" said Rick. Rick was the older one amongst the rest of the guys. Will, who was also Jamal's suitemate began to have a change of heart.

"We'll let him slide this time I guess", said Willie. Jamal, Derwin, Rick, and Will informed both officers that they decided to not press charges on Jimmy. Jimmy was released out of custody from campus safety.

"You better thank these gentlemen, because if it was me, you would've been spending your holiday in jail", said Officer Brooks.

"Thank you guys. I really do appreciate you. Again, I am so sorry", said Jimmy.

Chapter Fourteen

CLOSER TO GRADUATION

JAMAL WAS BACK IN SCHOOL for another semester with things going back to normal. He was also interested in joining Chill Beta Gamma, one of the well known frats on the yard. This was a social fraternity organization. Their colors were navy blue and silver. They had the best parties and were some cool, down-to-earth brothers. Also, Jamal was finally able to find a job. He worked as a telemarketer raising funds for police law enforcement organizations all across the state of South Carolina. Most of the employees that worked there had criminal backgrounds. However, this job also had a very high turnover rate. People would only work there for a few weeks and quit or get fired due to poor management and/or job abandonment. The money was good for Jamal's sake. He had no intentions on quitting at all.

He was also able to help get his former roommate Craig a job there as well. The two talked about becoming roommates again next semester One day after work, Jamal and Craig were riding with a friend Leroy in Leroy's girlfriend's car. Leroy was dropping the two gentlemen off at Jamal's dorm, which was off campus in a housing apartment complex. Leroy lived in an apartment off campus as well, but his apartment was no affiliation with Blakely College whatsoever. As he turned into the entrance of Jamal's off campus apartment, the college campus safety had it blocked off and were doing a search of all vehicles entering. The guys got so nervous as this was very unexpected and random.

"Yall just be cool and act normal," said Leroy.

The officers asked the gentlemen to step out of the car. They all were searched. The officers could smell marijuana on Leroy, which gave them reasonable doubt to search the car he was driving. There was a purse in the back on the floor. The officers opened the purse and found an ounce of marijuana. Jamal got super nervous. But unlike Ty, Leroy admitted that it belonged to him. Leroy also knew the law really well. He told officers that he smoked it which is considered a misdemeanor for a first-time offense. Since there were no smaller individual bags found, Leroy faced a charge of simple possession.

"It belongs to me", said Leroy.

"Yall need to watch who yall hang around with," said one of the officers.

"We didn't know, we were just being dropped off," said Craig.

"Yall had nothing to do with this, yall don't have explain anything to them," said Leroy. Then he asked the officers, "Can yall please hurry and take me to booking so I can call my lawyer and be bailed out by tonight?"

Officer Brooks pulled up on the scene thinking Jamal was busted again.

"Well, well, well...what do we have here again?" asked Officer Brooks.

Jamal didn't say anything to him, but just looked at Officer Brooks the same way actor Lawrence Fishburne looked at the black officer from the film *"Boyz n da Hood*[2]*"* after the burglary scene. Legendary director John Singleton featured this in the film to show that there are some black cops let their power go to their heads and will do anything to prove a point even to their own kind.

"I think you need to speak with your fellow officers before you start assuming," said Jamal.

The president of the SGA arrived as well, as a concerned SGA president should be. "Not you, Jamal. I'm not going to stand here and believe you have anything illegal on you," said the SGA president.

"I didn't do anything," said Jamal.

"Mr Jamal has two felony charges on his record," said Officer Brooks to the SGA president.

"Wow, so you really going to share my personal business like that?" asked Jamal.

---

[2] Boyz n da Hood is a coming of age film released in 1991, written and directed by the legendary John Singleton(1968-2019)

"Just shut up and be quiet," said Officer Brooks. He walked up to the other officers and they explained the situation to him. Jamal and Craig were free to go while Leroy was taken into custody. Leroy yelled out to Craig and Jamal, "Call my girl and tell her to get my car."

The very next day, the SGA president met with Jamal regarding what happened previously.

"There's been a lot of complaints about Officer Brooks. What he told me yesterday about your felony charges was none of my business and I thought that was very unprofessional. I have enough complaints to ask the board to have him removed from this campus," he told Jamal.

"I have no problem at all with that," Jamal replied. "However, what I do have a problem with is, I may not be able to get a decent job when I graduate due to this felony conviction on my record," he said.

Jamal explained the whole story of what happened to him when he got arrested.

"I can't get this expunged according to the state of South Carolina", said Jamal.

"Then get a pardon", he told him.

The only thing about a pardon is that the charge still remains on my record," said Jamal.

"Well, at least it's better than not getting one at all," said the SGA president.

As time went on, Jamal continued working and was able to earn enough money to join Chill Beta Gamma. He got the chance to learn more about his line brothers. While being on line, one of the rules was to not let anyone know what you were doing. Even though Craig and Jamal were still roommates, Jamal still had to keep it a secret about him being online. It was at such times that Craig got worried about Jamal. Jamal would always be either sleeping throughout the day or gone on the weekends and at night. One day, Craig asked Jamal, "You got someone pregnant or something?" "Nah, said Jamal as he chuckled at Craig's question.

One day while on line, while sitting in a small '92 Nissan Stanza, Jamal and his fellow line brothers waited to meet with their Dean of Pledges, Assistant Dean of Pledges, and big brothers; Jamal and his five other line brothers, Jayshaun, Lee, Anthony, Arthur, and Donell were discussing the things they regret from their past. Of course Jamal discussed his past incident. One of his line brothers had heard the same story.

"Wow, I didn't know that was you," said one of his line brothers.

Jamal explained how he was not able to get the charge removed from his record. They all felt sympathy for him, and encouraged him. Jamal could not believe that he would be pledging a frat with a felony conviction. There were no background check requirements. The night he ended hell week with his line brothers, he was able to tell Craig the truth why he was gone so much. It made more sense to Craig. Hell Week is supposedly to be the worst and hopefully final week of being on line joining the frat. Historically, some organizations have been kicked off campus while some members have been charged due to some pledgees who have been killed because of hazing. It's a reason why Jamal kept it a total secret from his roommate.

"I was about to call your parents on you," said Craig.

All Jamal could do was laugh. He invited Craig to come out to their probate show.

It was now time for Jamal and his line brothers to reveal themselves on campus. They had their probate show outside on campus. As Jamal was stepping, he could see both Mr Phillips and Officer Brooks standing right beside each other talking. It's a strong possibility that they're talking about me, Jamal thought. When it was time for the pledges to reveal themselves, Jamal made direct eye contact with Mr Phillips and Officer Brooks. Even during the step routines, his energy and adrenaline increased as the thought of being wrongfully accused of a crime that he didn't commit and being able to express this through his steps. Jamal kept on his pledge face. His mouth frowned but with a very angry look on his face. The audience cheered for Jamal and he became more popular on campus.

Chapter Fifteen

JAMAL AND TERRI

Jamal and the rest of his frat brothers traveled to many different college campuses going to tons of frat and sorority parties. They met a lot of different young women and sometimes visited them as well to spend weekends with them. One weekend while hanging out with some frat groupies, Jamal got a Facebook message from a girl named Terri who was in his Sociology class. She had a question regarding a homework assignment. Jamal replied indicating the instructions for the assignment, but was puzzled that she messaged him. Jamal had never spoken to her nor did he know anything about her. The next time Jamal saw Terri, he made sure to find out why she singled him out.

"Terri," said Jamal to get her attention. She looked at Jamal waiting for him to say something. "So did you get that assignment done?" he asked.

"Yeah, I sure did. Thanks," said Terri.

"Just out of curiosity, why did you message me?" asked Jamal.

"Well I noticed you take this class seriously and I also noticed that we were online since we're friends on facebook," said Terri.

Jamal still curious, thought of something to say real quick to keep the conversation going. "So where you from?" he asked.

"I'm from Atlanta," said Terri.

The two hit it off really well and started dating.

On one of their first dates, they ended up having dinner at an all night cafe. Terri decided to play a game with Jamal. It was like an ice breaker.

"With no judgement, we both have to tell each other something about us that we regret," she said.

In Jamal's mind, this was easy, but he wasn't sure if Terri could actually sit and remain judgment free. He took a deep breath as he chose to go first. He began by saying,

"Well, I regret that during my sophomore year, I allowed a group of guys in my room to smoke weed. This caused the dorm director, Mr Phillips, to inspect my room and call the campus public safety officers. They searched my room and found drugs hidden in my pillow. I really didn't know how they got there at the time."

"Wow, I'm speechless Jamal", said Terri.

"Well, it's definitely nothing I'm proud of, Jamal said.

"Everyone makes mistakes in life. You haven't been in anymore trouble have you", she asked Jamal.

"Of course not. My family would probably disown me", said Jamal

"Don't be so hard on yourself. There's people out there with worst things on their record. So what are you doing to correct this", asked Terri.

"Since I'm not eligible for an expungement, I wonder if a pardon will actually work since the charge still remains; there's still a possibility that I might not get it. I need three good references to speak on my behalf who will not expose my past," said Jamal.

"If you're worried about them exposing your past, then they're probably not good references to speak on your behalf to begin with. What other choice do you have?" Terri asked.

"I can start my own business," he said.

"And how's that going so far?" Terri asked.

With nothing left to say, Jamal thought about filming a documentary about the whole incident.

"Maybe I could attend film school after graduation," said Jamal since his major was Broadcast Journalism.

"That's great Jamal. I believe you can do it. Just don't forget about your pardon. Without it, it could hold you back from that good job that's going to allow you to save up the money for your next video project", Terri said.

Before they ended the night, Jamal said, "Hey, we never talked about what you regretted."

Terri paused…"Well, the one thing I regret is dating a police officer," she said.

"Wait, what?" asked Jamal.

They continued their discussion later on the phone. Terri finally told Jamal what happened between her and the police she dated. She revealed to him that it was Officer Brooks. Jamal was really shocked. He couldn't believe it.

"He's the officer who took me to jail," said Jamal.

"I'm not surprised at all" Terri said.

"So you were dating a jerk huh", asked Jamal

"Well, it didn't started that way. I thought he could protect me. We kept things private away from campus, but I started to notice an abusive side of him. Then I just ended it with him. He started stalking me, I reported him and he's no longer an officer here", said Terri.

"Wow, I remember me and the SGA president having a conversation about him. He, was telling me they were trying to get rid of him" said Jamal. Jamal and Terri remained friends, but Jamal kept his distance as he wanted to focus more on himself.

Chapter Sixteen

GEARING UP FOR GRADUATION

It was finally the last semester of college for Jamal. However, Jamal wasn't quite aware at first. He knew he had to take 17 hours plus two more extra hours because of a continuation of two of his courses. His hardest course was Technical Writing, which was taught by his advisor, Dr Greggs. So Jamal had to make sure that he passed this class. He refused to fail his own advisor's class.

"It doesn't make sense to come back next semester for only two hours. I'm going to get permission from the dean to see if you can take your two part courses all together in one semester," said Dr Greggs.

Jamal was excited as he shared the good news with his frat brothers and his parents.

He still had his job as a telemarketer. As a college student and working part-time, things seemed a bit promising for him. He was thankful that he was able to get hired despite his criminal background. But life after college in pursuit of a better job seemed a little impossible. Most of the good jobs required a background check and most Fortune 500 companies aren't hiring convicts. Jamal felt safe that he would work his current job until he found something better.

Terri still supported and motivated Jamal. She looked past his felony record and his possible future. She knew his best option at this point would be to get a pardon.

"Have you worked on that pardon yet?" asked Terri.

Jamal answered, "Not yet."

"Well, what are you waiting for?" Terri asked.

"Classes are really weighing on me and I'm just trying to focus on graduating", said Jamal.

"Okay, I'll take your word. But the only person or thing that's holding you back is you. I'm just saying…" she concluded.

As a Broadcast Journalism major, Jamal had the opportunity for a temporary internship. A national TV network was doing a special on HBCU campuses. Each week they'd visit an HBCU. The professors in the department did an evaluation on each student whom they thought would be a good fit. Only three were selected for a paid internship and Jamal was one that got chosen. He felt highly honored. He thought to himself, "Would a person with a criminal felony on their record ever get such an opportunity?" Thoughts like this always came to mind for Jamal.

The name of the TV special was *HBCU Showcase: Life Within the Quad*. It was Jamal's job to assist the casting director. Jamal enjoyed every bit of it. He had a say on which students got filmed on the show. During the pre-production as well as production, Jamal got excused from his classes. Although, he had a chance to have some fun and learn some new exciting things, this sort of put him a little behind with his assignments. Not to mention, he had to put in time for his fraternity.

Jamal was extremely busy. As soon as the first day of production, Jamal had to attend a very important mandatory meeting with his fraternity brothers. Meanwhile, after production of the show was done, there was also a brief meeting about how things went so far as the recent shoot.

"Has anyone seen Jamal?" one of the producers asked. No one knew. But in actuality, Jamal vanished after the shoot to attend his fraternity meeting then headed for work afterwards. Jamal's fraternity was in the process of working on a very impactful community service project.

The next day for the shoot, all of Jamal's co-interns informed him of what happened previously.

"Where were you? The producers were looking for you," said one of the other interns.

"I had a very important meeting that I needed to attend", Jamal said.

The director walked up to Jamal. "Are you Jamal?" he asked. "I heard some bad things about you yesterday. You didn't attend our meeting after the shoot. What was that about?" he asked.

"I had to attend another meeting," Jamal said nervously. The internship was important, but also was the meeting with his fraternity.

"We're going to have to take you off the payroll," said the director.

Although, Jamal was stripped from payroll, he still had his telemarketing job and he was still able to gain experience from the internship.

As the overall production wrapped up, Jamal gave his resume to one of the producers, Tim.

"Thank you. Here's my card," said Tim.

He also gave Jamal a list of all of the workers who worked on the production along with their contact information. These workers ranged from executives, camera operators, directors, producers, casting team members, make-up, caterers, etc.

"If you have any questions or need some help with anything, don't hesitate to hit me up," Tim said.

By the time midterms came, Jamal was barely passing. He had completed the one-week internship. He requested for a leave of absence from his job to focus on his studies. Surprisingly, they granted it to him.

During Jamal's last few weeks of classes, he studied very hard. He spent most of his time in the library or computer lab reading and working on his assignments. The final week of class, Jamal found out he passed all of his classes except for Technical Writing. Dr Greggs gave all the graduating seniors instructions on how to view their final grades of the course- Technical Writing via Blackboard at 6 pm. Jamal nervously waited for 6 pm. He accessed the blackboard app on his phone. However, when he tried to open up Dr Gregg's message, he got a message stating that in order to read the message, he needs to view it from a computer desktop or laptop. So, he rushed to the nearest computer lab on campus. Once he opened up the message from Dr Greggs, it read: "Sorry students for the inconvenience. Unfortunately, I was unable to send your final grade via blackboard. Instead I left them on the door at my office. You'll see them inside the envelope with the last 4 numbers of your social security number. Look for your envelope with your last 4 SS#. If you passed, congratulations.

If not, I'll see you again next semester for I'm the only professor who teaches this course."

Jamal ran to Dr Greggs' office. When he got to the door, he paused for a quick prayer, took a deep breath, and began searching for his envelope with the last 4 digits of his social security number. He eventually found it. Nervously he opened it up and his final grade average was a 79, which meant he passed and will be graduating. He was totally excited. He called his parents to relay the good news.

He also told Terri. She was happy for him and told him that this was the perfect time to get his pardon. At the very moment, Jamal didn't want to think about it because he was more interested in celebrating his success of graduating from college.

Chapter Seventeen

THE COUNTY JAIL VISIT

Jamal met with his fraternity brothers once more regarding the new graduates including himself and more information about their upcoming community service project. The project was meant to educate the young incarcerated inmates in the county jail. Jamal felt this would be a good opportunity to encourage those prisoners who especially are first-time felons or wrongfully accused. This gave him a chance to tell his story.

Jamal and his frat brothers made it on site to the county jail. They were given a tour and it looked just like how it looked on TV. Some inmates threatened them while some tried to intimidate them as they walked through the prison cell hallways.

One inmate yelled out, "Man yall some ##########!" But Jamal and his frat brothers gave no reaction nor did they make eye contact. When it was time to gather all the inmates, Jamal along with each of his fraternity brothers prepared themselves to speak.

The first speaker to represent the fraternity was brother David Atkins, a prominent graduate of Bazemore College and a successful lawyer. He spoke about his experience of working with ex convicts helping them get back on track with their lives. He stated that, " Some wants what's best for them, some just want to settle and in some cases that may not be such a bad thing, but others just want to end up back in prison. Which individual are you? Everyone should want what's best for them, but not everyone is willing to do what it takes in order get what's best for them."

The next speaker was Jamal's big brother, Tory Case. Tory still had a few classes left in order to graduate, but he told the story of how he had to get away from his environment by all means necessary. Tory grew up in a very rough neighborhood.

"I started gangbanging at the age of 12 and was a drug dealer by age 14. When I was 16, I even started robbing people, but eventually got caught and was sent to juvenile prison. Luckily, the judge gave me another chance", said Tory. He also talked about how he got his GED from Job Corps and later enrolled at a technical college.

"Two years later, I transferred to Bazemore College and enlisted in the Air Force Reserves. The prisoners gave him a standing ovation when he ended his speech. It was filled with motivation and taught that your past doesn't determine your future. Your present does.

Up next was Jamal. As he started speaking, he noticed one of the inmates. Jamal recognized that the inmate was Ty—the same person who Jamal was going to talk about in his story. Jamal talked about his life growing up. He came from a good family with a good background. His only and worst mistake was allowing "so-called" friends in his dorm to smoke weed. When Jamal mentioned this, a tear trickled down Ty's face. Jamal told the same story as he always had. He also talked about how it would be difficult for him to find a good job with his record.

"But keep in mind guys, depending on the severity of your offense, you still may be able to get an expungement. If not, there's also something called a pardon. It'll help as well," said Jamal to the prison audience.

They applauded after Jamal finished speaking. Once all the speaking was done, the fraternity brothers were able to speak on an individual basis with some of the prisoners.

Jamal approached Ty as soon as he got a chance. They both stood and stared at each other for an endless moment.

"Is it really you?" asked Ty.

"Yes it really is me," said Jamal.

"You did a good job with the speech," Ty said.

"Thanks," Jamal replied.

"Look, I'm sorry for what happened. I should've claimed that weed," he said.

"It's in the past now. Nothing we can do about it," said Jamal.

Jamal admitted he still hadn't gotten over it, but he realized now was a good opportunity to forgive him, although it was hard to forget what Ty did. They shook hands and hugged.

"By the way, what are you doing here?" asked Jamal.

"To make a long story short, the very next semester I decided to take a break from school. I continued to sell weed and eventually karma caught up with me. I got greedy, then I got lazy. Once I got lazy, I became too comfortable. Obviously, the cops were watching me and my supplier. I got caught and was arrested. My supplier was able to get his charges dropped. The judge told me since I wasn't in school anymore, I should be behind bars instead. Again I'm sorry," Ty said.

"Why didn't you apply for PTI?" asked Jamal.

"I had too much weight on me", said Ty.

Jamal realized Ty had the same exact charge as Jamal, but Jamal did not had to serve any time for it. Jamal realized how blessed he was.

Brother David Atkins pulled Jamal to the side to discuss his charge.

"Brother Williams, you graduate next week, right?" he asked.

Jamal says, "Yes sir, in fact I do."

"We're going to have to do something about your record," said brother David. "Since you're ineligible for an expungement, allow me to help you with getting your pardon," he said.

The next week, Jamal earned his Bachelor of Arts degree in Broadcast Journalism as he walked with his graduating class.

Chapter Eighteen

LIFE AFTER BAZEMORE COLLEGE

Jamal was given more than enough advice to earn a pardon for his conviction. Brother David Atkins told him to not mention that he's innocent.

"In their eyes, you're still guilty no matter what. So far as your pardon, contact some really good positive people who can speak highly of you of you on behalf", said Brother David Atkins.

Meanwhile Jamal contiued his job as a telemarketer, but unfortunately the company was laying off all of their old employees. This meant Jamal had to move back home to live with his parents. Jamal had a plan though. He focused on what was needed in order to get his pardon. Knowing that he needed references to speak on his behalf, he was very skeptical as to whom else he would share his past to. His father set up a meeting for Jamal with a well known senator from their hometown. As Jamal began to explain the story of his infamous arrest at Bazemore College, Senator Alcorn immediately interrupted Jamal to inform him about getting an expungement.

"I've already done my research and I'm ineligible for an expungement, because of the type of felony that the charge was classified as," said Jamal.

"You gotta be kidding me," said Senator Alcorn.

Jamal and his father were surprised, because not even the senator was aware of the state laws.

"How can a person better themselves if they can't get a mistake removed from their record? This upsets me, Mr Williams", said Senator Alcorn

"There's two things we would like to discuss. First of all, we know he's not able to get an expungement. Therefore, are you willing to write a letter on his behalf so he can at least get a pardon," asked Mr Williams.

Senator Alcorn agreed.

"Secondly, is there a way that this law can be changed?" said Jamal. "I was young and didn't know what I was doing, and not to mention, they denied me PTI because due to the fact that it happened at Bazemore College."

Senator Alcorn stated that he would get together along with his fellow colleagues to make a proposal to see what could be done about changing this law code. Jamal was able to get a letter of reference from him as well for his pardon application, but he still needed two more.

Chapter Nineteen

FILM SCHOOL, UNEMPLOYMENT BENEFITS, AND A PARDON

Eventually, Jamal was able to get unemployment benefits. He still had dreams about going to film school and shooting a documentary based on his story of being wrongfully accused. He applied to a film school with a college campus so he could have somewhere to live. It meant he would have roommates, but with a felony record, it was hard for him to find his own apartment.

He also finally applied for his pardon. However, it would take one year for an individual to be eligible for a pardon after the application is submitted, which is the same length of time in order to complete the film school program.

Everything worked out on perfect timing. Jamal was able to attend film school. By the time he completes the film school program, it will be time for him to attend the Pardon hearing and appear in front of the Parole, Probation, and Pardon Board. Not to mention, his only income came from unemployment benefits which also only lasted a year. Unfortunately he could not get food stamps since some states ruled that if you have a felony, you're ineligible for government food assistance thanks to the Clinton Administration.

While in film school, Jamal got a Facebook phone call from a high school classmate by the name of Darren Rogers. It appeared that Darren was assisting Senator Alcorn's campaign for re-election. A little puzzled about why Darren would call him since the two hardly ever spoke to each other in high school. Darren had the reputation of associating with individuals whom he could manipulate for his advantage. He earned his degree in Marketing from an HBCU as well, South Chatman University of Business. With a business in real estate, Darren was very successful for his age. Reluctantly, Jamal answered.

"Hey Jamal, quick question. You're in film school, right?" Darren asked.

"Why, yes."

"The reason I'm asking is because of the re-election for Senator Alcorn. We would like to add you on staff as our Communications Specialist," said Darren.

Jamal's first thoughts were kind of odd. Everyone knows how wealthy and successful Darren is and if he really wanted a professional, he could've hired someone else with a lot more experience.

"I'm just an unemployed film student with a criminal drug felony," Jamal thought.

But then again, the thought of him having this opportunity was a blessing in disguise. Truthfully, Darren could afford to hire a video professional with a lot more experience than Jamal. But the reason he decided to choose Jamal was because they both were from the hometown and attended the same high school. Nothing like being from a small town where everyone knows you. So, when you move away, and then come back to visit, people treat you like a well known celebrity. This was definitely how Darren was treated whenever he came to visit. He was able to take a leave of absence while Senator Alcorn compensated him very well to assist in his campaign. Just maybe this would also give him an opportunity to have Darren as a second reference for his pardon.

Jamal and Terri kept in contact. While Jamal was in film school, Terri was working on her Masters. They were in separate states so they did plenty of video chatting, maintaining a long distance relationship. Terri served as his motivation to succeed.

In one of his projects in film school, Jamal had to write a treatment script for a documentary. Of course Jamal already knew what he was going to do. He wrote about the effects of being wrongfully accused when there's nothing much you can do about it. He researched statistics and talked about the procedures of obtaining an expungement. He also explained that different states have different ways of granting their pardons.

For example, in the state of Michigan, only the governor grants pardons. But luckily, all Jamal had to do in the state of South Carolina was apply by writing a statement letter on why he should be granted a pardon and have three references write a letter on his behalf. He would then show up in front of the Board to plead his reason for being pardoned.

Jamal's instructor was intrigued by his documentary proposal. This prompted Jamal to schedule an appointment with Senator Alcorn to be a part of this documentary as well. Unfortunately due to the election, Senator Alcorn was far too busy to discuss Jamal's film school project at the time.

Jamal completed the documentary without the help of Senator Alcorn. Later, he discovered that Senator Alcorn had passed away due to a heart attack. Not only was this for a grade, but he felt that his story needed to be told. Time was winding down for Jamal to go to speak to the Parole, Probation, and Pardon Board and his graduation from film school was just a few days away.

Jamal got a phone call unexpectedly from Donovan.

"Who is this?" asked Jamal since the phone call came from an unknown number.

"It's me, Donovan," said Donovan.

The two hadn't talked since Jamal went back to school after his suspension. Donovan understood why Jamal might've avoided him.

"It wasn't intentional to avoid you," said Jamal.

"Look I understand. As a child I done childish things. I'm a man now and I put down all my childish ways", said Donovan.

"What are you saying", said Jamal.

"I'm a changed man now. I've changed my old ways. I'm here to be a better man and encouraged those out there who may still be lost like I once was. I'd like you to meet someone real soon", said Donovan.

"That's good to hear. My pardon hearing is tomorrow and it's at the state capital building.," said Jamal.

"That's perfect, we can meet you there," said Donovan.

Would you like to attend and speak on my behalf?" asked Jamal.

"Absolutely, it'll be an honor," Donovan answered.

Chapter Twenty

THE PARDON HEARING

Jamal drove about three hours in order to make it to the state capital building. Also attending the hearing was Brother David Atkins, as well as Jamal's father. The more good people who could speak on Jamal's behalf, the higher the possibility of him getting pardoned. Jamal met with everyone

"I already know this guy," said Jamal's dad towards Donovan.

"I thought you said you were bringing someone," said Jamal to Donovan.

"They're on their way," said Donovan.

The pardon hearings are first come first serve. There were about 10 people ahead of Jamal. The lobby was crowded, but as time got closer, each offender along with his or her guests had to move around to different rooms in order to be called upon for their individual hearing.

Donovan and Jamal discussed how life's been treating them. Jamal talked about the documentary that he completed.

"It's going to be epic," said Jamal, the excitement evident in his voice. Donovan liked the idea of it. "So enough about me, what's up with you?" he said.

"Well, I had a wake-up call," said Donovan. "I almost got killed and I could've gone to prison for a very long time," Donovan continued.

The time was winding down and Jamal was told that he should see the board in about 20 minutes. Donovan immediately got out his seat to step outside the lobby area with his phone in his hand.

The time was getting closer and closer, but Donovan still hadn't returned.

"He said he was bringing someone else to speak on my behalf, but I don't have a clue to who he's talking about," said Jamal.

The party right before Jamal went next. Once they're finished, Jamal and his guests would have their chance to go. Still no sign of Donovan. As the group that went before Jamal exited, Jamal and his guests were called to go next.

"We may have to go without them," said Jamal's father.

"I agree," said brother David Atkins.

"Jamal Williams," yelled out by one of the coordinators.

Jamal stood up to notify that he was Mr Jamal Williams.

"Are these all of your guests?" asked the coordinator.

Before Jamal could say anything, Donovan returned. Not only did he return, he also brought the guest whom he had been referring to. Jamal was speechless, but it was time for him and his guests to go inside the room with board members. The board director spoke to Jamal and his guests.

"Please introduce your guests," said the board director. "This is my father, Mr James Williams. This is my frat brother, Mr David Atkins. Two friends of mine, Mr Donovan Montgomery and Mr Tyrone…" said Jamal.

Ty finished his last name by saying, "Bryce."

"Sorry, Mr Tyrone Bryce," said Jamal.

Jamal was nervous, emotional, and a little confused at the same time. He could not figure out the connection between Donovan and Ty.

His dad was first to speak.

"Jamal definitely deserved a second chance. He finished college and will graduate film school very soon. Why not allow him to be a productive citizen?" said Jamal's dad. He also went to say that, "Me and my wife raised Jamal from love. When this incident happened, he was a young college student. It was a mistake that shouldn't have never happened. If he doesn't get pardoned, there's no possible way for him to truly enjoy his life with all of the abundancy.

Up next was brother David Atkins. He talked about Jamal's upcoming documentary film as well as Jamal's positive attitude while as an undergrad student at Bazemore College. "I was surprised that he even had a record.

That goes to show you that this is charge on his record is not who Jamal is," said brother David Atkins.

Then it was time for Donovan to speak.

"First off, I would like to say that this young man is someone whom I look up to even though I'm older. I admire the fact that he took the initiative to go to college despite getting suspended. He went back and still graduated. That says a lot about his character. When I heard what happened I was furious, because I know it wasn't all Jamal's fault. I myself had a run in with the law, but that was before I turned my life around. That's how I met this young man," said Donovan as he pointed towards Ty. Jamal was speechless. Ty stood up and asked if he could speak.

"Go ahead sir," said the director of pardon, parole, and probation.

"I was so scared, I didn't know what to do. At the time, it was either my freedom or someone else's. All I have to say is this man is innocent of the crime he was charged with. I was the one whom those drugs belonged to," said Ty.

The board was speechless and shocked.

"Mr Williams, if you don't have anything else to say, we can go ahead and deliberate and give you our decision in about five minutes.

"I would like to say that when this incident occurred, I was young, I was childish, and I was very naive. Over the years, this arrest has taught me so much. I don't plan on having any more run ins with the law," said Jamal.

One of the board members wanted to say something to Jamal. "Mr Williams, you do realize this was a very serious crime. I mean that was a lot of marijuana they found on you. People have served prison time for that exact crime. I just want you think about that before we give you our decision," she said.

Jamal and his guests were asked to step out of the room. Patiently waiting for the outcome, Brother David asked Ty would he be willing to confess if Jamal decides to re-open the case.

"I'll do anything to make my wrong right," said Ty.

"So, how do you two know each other again", asked Jamal.

"Ty was one of my sellers. The cops were watching me the whole time. After making a trip to Ty, the cops followed me, but found no drugs. They did found an unregistered gun I had and one of them did almost shot me so they dropped all charges. Unfortunately, they still had a warrant on Ty", said Donovan.

As for Ty, he was sent to jail. This gave him a lot of time to think. He realized he should've admit that the drugs found in Jamal's pillow belonged to him.

The coordinator came out to finally announce to Jamal that the board's decision was to grant Jamal his pardon.

"Congratulations Mr Williams. You will get your Pardon Certificate in a week from today," said the coordinator.

Everyone cheered!

Jamal's father was extremely happy and proud as he thanked all who showed up.

"Hey young man, I never officially met you, but for a long time, I really did despise you. Today I'm thankful that you took time out of your busy schedule to speak on my son's behalf," Jamal's dad said to Ty.

"Thanks, you know for a long time I dealt with my conscience eating me up alive to the point it took me selling drugs and living life on the edge just so I wouldn't think about I what I did to your son. It came back around to me and I actually did time for it. Today I feel better even though I'm willing to have Jamal's case reopened so I can confess to the felony that I should've been charged for a few years ago," said Ty.

Brother David gave Ty his business card. "It's going to take a while, but we can get this done. This time you won't get any jail time. I promise you that," he said.

"Mercy has been finally granted to you my brother, congratulations," said Donovan.

"Thanks," said Jamal.

Jamal let Terri know the great news and she was happy for him.

Chapter Twenty-One
DESERVING MERCY

One year later, Jamal's case got turned over to Tyrone Bryce aka Ty. He got sentenced to one year-probation just like Jamal did a few years ago. Jamal not only got a public apology from the county, but also from Bazemore College. The college offered to pay off his entire student loan debt, including film school.

Jamal cultivated a business relationship with Tim, the producer of HBCU Showcase. After that Jamal's story got social media attention, and he started to get phone calls and emails from many journalists and producers interested in hearing his story. He also had a legal meeting with the PR Department at Bazemore College regarding his documentary and any future media opportunities as it related to the brand of the college. He began speaking at high schools and churches encouraging students to not be a victim of peer pressure. Tim helped him with getting his documentary produced. Jamal appeared on TV/radio shows across the country.

Jamal enjoyed this stage of his career and life. He and Terri were no longer in a long distance relationship. They were finally engaged to be married. He got offers from many big universities to teach Film and Media. Although Bazemore College paid him back and more, he received an offer to teach there also.

His documentary was groundbreaking, just as he predicted. Everyone thought it was very interesting. Not only was Jamal was able to tell his story, but it sparked an interest from many politicians and lawmakers.

Prison reform became a major topic in the community because many people started to realize that some of the laws were designed for people of a certain class to fail.

If only Jamal did not allow those guys in his dorm room. If only Jamal would've told those cops that those drugs belonged to one of the other guys and not him (although he actually didn't know who the drugs belonged to at the very moment), then just maybe none of this would've happened to Jamal. None of these unfortunate events would have occurred. But if they never occurred, maybe he wouldn't have been able to tell this story of how he was arrested for something he was innocent of. His misfortune had given him fame and success. Jamal's nightmare was finally over. He received mercy, which had been very deserving…Deserving Mercy. Deserving is justice.

Deserving Mercy's Short Book of Poetry:
Poetry inspired by this story

They Don't Know, Only God Does

They don't know what it feels like to be blamed. Falsely accused.
Putting dirt on your name. Now I feel so ashamed.

I can't even walk straight without feeling some kind of way.
My frustration goes back and forth. I'm a young black man so going to counseling is out of the question.
We don't do that in our community. But that's another discussion

Back to the matter of fact.
Where was the discernment ever taken ever taken into consideration?
No one thought about or strategic investigation?
No one thought about the media?

No one could've predicted the me too now movement. But this is not about that movement. This is about me finally being mature enough to deal with my own skeletons hidden in my closet. Time to clean it out!

Jamal's Prayer

Dear Lord,
Forgive me for my sin of allowing and partaking in an act that I had no business partaking in. Forgive everyone involved. Help me to forgive the one who be trayed and allowed me to be accused of a crime that I did not commit. Father, you know the truth. Let the truth set me free in the eyes of you as well as the eyes of man. Allow me to forgive the dorm director, as he was only doing his job. Allow me to forgive the officers involved, as they were just doing their also, but not realizing how or who's life they're contributing to be ruined. If they do know, Lord please have mercy on their soul. Finally, I asked you Lord that I be fully redeemed from this unfortunate matter. I pray that this prayer will lead to the action of forgiving. Lord you know how hard this is, but I ask for your Grace and Mercy. Heal me and let your greatness be manifested especially to the ones that were tested.
Amen.

Dear Officer Brooks

Dear Officer Brooks, looks like I'm in a bad situation. Worst than I thought.
I'll never forget that night when I was so called caught.
But if I dwell too long on this thought. I'll become furious as I think of a plot. Instead, I'll be like Mr Spock.
Use no emotion for commotion. Just sit back and watch.

Sitting back and just watching got me into more trouble.
But only if you knew exactly what I went through.
You'd know it was all a struggle. There's no progress without it. Expungement? Yeah I doubt it.

Pre Trial Intervention also known as PTI, was nothing but a joke, a scam, dishonor and a lie. I shouldn't be surprise that I was denied. You owe me, Officer Brooks. Goodbye.

About the Book

HAVE YOU EVER YOU BEEN accused of something you didn't do? Meet Jamal. Jamal is a young black man in college who ends up hanging with the wrong crowd. Little does he know while being careless and naive, a "so called friend" allows him to take the blame for a serious crime. For now on, all odds are against Jamal. Could there be a way out for him?

This book reveals truth that takes place on the campuses of Historically Black Colleges and/or Universities (HBCUs). It also reflects on how unfair the judicial system is, especially to minorities.

www.ingramcontent.com/pod-product-compliance
Lightning Source LLC
LaVergne TN
LVHW011732060526
838200LV00051B/3152